A JOURNEY OF REMEMBERING

While Seeking the Ultimate Love

NATHAN WHITING

ISBN: 978-0-9824870-3-7

Copyright 2010 by Nathan Whiting

All rights reserved. Except for use in any review, the reproduction or utilization of this work in whole or in part in any form by any electronic, mechanical or other means, now known or hereafter invented, including xerography, photocopying and recording, or in any information storage or retrieval system, is forbidden without the written permission of the publisher, Summerland Publishing, 21 Oxford Drive, Lompoc, CA 93436.

Printed in the United States of America.

Library of Congress #: 2010923003

Acknowledgements

I would like to wholeheartedly thank all of my fellow journeyers who've made this great adventure possible. There's a famous cliché that goes like this: *You don't know what you have until it's gone.* I consider myself one of the fortunate few who've been blessed to realize what I have right now, before it's too late. Right now I am blessed with living twenty years past what I figured I ever would, because I *knew* I would never see the age of thirty with the lifestyle I was living at the time. Right now I am eternally grateful for being a recovered alcoholic and drug addict who is able to share with others some of the "golden nuggets" of spirituality I have stumbled upon throughout this journey of remembering. Right now I am eternally grateful to the Great Spirit for his/her compassion, kindness, and truly unconditional love with no strings attached. It's through your grace that I'm able to express this unconditional love to all others I meet on the path of remembering.

This personal journey of remembering would never have been possible without the major and minor characters that have so lovingly shared this lifetime with me. I've been blessed with people who even though I trashed them in a sense, have found it in their hearts to forgive my transgressions and not hold them against me. These people know who they are and don't need to be named. I thank you for your kindness, patience, understanding, and most of all, your love.

For my other spiritual masters who've come and offered guidance to me on the path of remembering, what can I say? "Thank you" is not nearly enough. I am expressing my appreciation of your time, talents, gifts, love, and Kleenexes by sharing my life's adventure with the next searching soul who stumbles onto the path of remembering.

Most of all, I would like to say "Thank you" for not letting go of my hand and keeping your belief in me alive! Stealing a line from my two-year-old granddaughter "Pumpkin," I say to *all* who've joined me throughout the years since coming into this plane of existence: ***"I love you soooo much!"***

FORWARD

This is my story of a self-induced journey into and through hell, on my way to finding and remembering a way "home" and stumbling upon the ultimate love that is unconditional in form. While preparing for this journey of remembering, I found myself conscience enough at times to realize and save the gold nuggets of spirituality I came upon, hoping one day to share these with others. While the gold nuggets are spiritual in nature, it's a raw variety of street spirituality. Being a non-conformist and rebel at heart, I had to find some type of spirituality that would work for me and get me back on the path of re-membering what I'm here for in the human form. This is a brutally honest (and sometimes graphic) retelling of this journey of recovery.

While seeking shelter from the storms I produced in my life, I caught a glimpse of a far-off light that offered hope and comfort for a safe landing on some distant and unrecognizable shore. What I have experienced does not seem all that different from many other fellow travelers who've taken it upon themselves to journey alone into the unknown sea of life. Most of the current generation of people has grown up being taught the traditional and conformist ways of their parents and grandparents, which the present generation finds lacking in some vital areas. Where is the true unconditional love and acceptance that is supposed to be offered by well-meaning theologies of today? Are we truly "our brother's keeper" or is this just a nice motto that gets a picture frame and hangs on a den wall? If we are all truly of one body, why do we insist on committing suicide in a sense? It's with questions such as these that "rebels" are retreating from the old attitudes of the past and embracing a more compassionate way of living, laughing, and loving.

If you care to journey along with me on this path I've chosen, you're more than welcome to come along. First off, this journey is about re-membering your true nature (which is based on freedom) and secondly, this journey practices the truest form of love which is totally unconditional at its core; a core that has no strings attached and no agenda to prove. Join me in accepting this offer of a new and wondrous way of living as we join others on the path. A great spiritual master once advised me to live my life out loud and with purpose. I'll never forget that nugget of spirituality. Thank you Master.

Table of Contents

CHAPTER 1: CHOOSING A PATH 1
CHAPTER 2: POWERLESSNESS 5
CHAPTER 3: SPIRITUALITY 8
CHAPTER 4: CONCEPTIONS OF GOD 14
CHAPTER 5: THE GREATER PLAN 18
CHAPTER 6: ALLOWING GOD IN THE DOOR. 23
CHAPTER 7: DEFINING WHO WE ARE 27
    Morals: *29*
    Resentments: *32*
    Fears: *34*
    Weaknesses: *36*
    Strengths: *39*
    Hopes & Dreams: *41*
CHAPTER 8: TURNING DEBITS INTO ASSETS 43
CHAPTER 9: SHARING OUR LIFE'S STORY 48
CHAPTER 10: BEING READY FOR THE HIGHER POWER 57
CHAPTER 11: CLEANING UP THE PAST 63
CHAPTER 12: YEARNING FOR LEARNING 74
CHAPTER 13: PARAMETERS OF GOD 78
CHAPTER 14: BEINGNESS 83
CHAPTER 15: MIRACLES 91
CHAPTER 16: SEEING THE BIG PICTURE 103
CHAPTER 17: PRAYER 109
CHAPTER 18: MEDITATION 119

CHAPTER 19: GOD IS IN THE *ALL* OF IT. 138
CHAPTER 20: QUIT WORRYING, START WONDERING! 148
CHAPTER 21: GRACE IN OUR LIVES. 155
CHAPTER 22: AN ATTITUDE OF GRATITUDE. 164
CHAPTER 23: A JOURNEY WELL TRAVERSED 173
ABOUT THE AUTHOR 180

A Journey of Remembering

CHAPTER 1: CHOOSING A PATH

Never a journey so far and wide will ever compare to the journey inside. What a journey it has been! My quest for meaning and purpose to my life began in earnest about nineteen years ago. I was at the point where I'd reached the end of the road that I chose to travel. The path I chose up to that point led me to a literal hell for myself and all the loved ones around me. There was no sanity to be had by anyone. It was survival of the fittest in my home. To be sure, it was everyone for themselves and the end result was our instincts were in constant collision with each other. It seemed the more I fought for my own sanity, the more it pushed others to fight for theirs, and when people are fighting for survival, sanity goes right out the window. I can remember saying to myself many times, "I'll do whatever I have to do to survive, screw everyone else!" Well, that's exactly what I ended up doing, screwing everyone (myself included).

Self-will or survival-will was the crux of the problem. When survival-will flares up in your life, it causes the will of others around you to flare up as well, and in here steps controversy. At this time, everyone will begin to fight as their own survival-wills dictate, for the self or ego of each one is in a fight for survival. Also figuring into the equation is the part of our self called "soul" which is searching to find its purpose in life. Since the soul is searching for purpose and the self is fighting for survival, and there is usually no direction or help in these pursuits, it's bound to put us into constant collision with those about us. There is no rhyme or reason to life and the result will be a string of self-imposed crises from which we're always trying to extradite ourselves, but to no avail.

Upon seeing survival-will is of no avail, where do we turn? We need to begin to look beyond it for the answers. It's through this process of looking beyond ourselves that we'll ultimately have to turn and look inside. This is where all answers will come from because that's where God is found. All answers lie in a Power greater than us, or our own survival-will.

Lack of the proper power is our dilemma. This writing is about how to acquire and use this power. Expressed in its simplest terms, that power is the power to give and receive unconditional positive regard for our world, its people, and ourselves; in other words, *to love all unconditionally.*

With the first few faltering steps on this new path, I had to have answers to questions that influenced my life so dramatically up to this point. They were questions such as these: What was this life all about? Was life meant to be just a lot of hurt, pain, and confusion, intermixed with a triumph or two? Are we born to live a life of seemingly unconnected coincidences and accidents and then die? What comes after we die? Is it heaven, hell, or oblivion? What's the human race here for anyway? Who or what is God? Could there really be a loving God behind this mayhem of a society of ours?

And so my search began. A lot of what my parents, religion, and society taught me just weren't working very well. I was taught you grow up, get a good job, start a family, and be true to God and everything will be relatively fine, and then you die. It's at the point of death when you better start hoping you haven't screwed things up too bad and you're headed in the right direction (meaning heaven or hell). These guidelines didn't seem to work for me. There had to be more than just these signposts as I traveled the road of life. Maybe that definition of life works for some people, but it wasn't working for me. I hoped life would be different when, with only the clothes on my back, I was forced to flee my parents' house when I was seventeen, but life was still pretty much the same.

I always felt I didn't fit in with things. Religion seemed to ask for perfection and nothing less, and I guess the same thing could be said of my parents. As much as I wanted to enjoy life, life and I just didn't seem to get along and I didn't know the answers on how to fix it; I didn't even know where to go to find the answers. The only thing I figured out was *I* was playing a major role in why life was not working

A Journey of Remembering

out for me.

We all have personal or soul issues to deal with, and a lot of these issues come from our upbringing or lack thereof. "So as the twig is bent, so grows the tree" is a very common phrase we've all heard, and so I've grown like the small tree - crooked. I was a so-called victim of my upbringing. I blamed external circumstances (religion, parents, kids in school, and God) for the life I had. Never once did I take responsibility for myself or my life. Playing the victim role leads to a loveless life which results in no love shown and none received.

"It's not my fault" is what I felt at the time when life seemed to have cornered me for some unknown reason. I'd scream, "It's the physical and mental torture my parents put me through and its society's fault for letting it continue!" closely followed by "It's the church which doesn't care." In the end, I just figured it was all God's fault. When we see ourselves as victims, we absolve ourselves of all responsibility to do anything about it. The thinking goes like this: *They* screwed me up and *they* have to make it right or to hell with them. I guess I'll just do whatever I have to do to survive.

But are we all victims? Yes and no. According to Webster's Dictionary, one of the definitions for the word victim is: *a person who suffers.* We all suffer at times in our lives and so yes, we're all victims. Firstly, do we have to suffer and secondly, if we do, must we stay that way? You will be a victim for as long as you choose to remain a victim. That is your choice and believe me, it is your choice. A person who suffers feels great amounts of pain. Pain is inevitable, but suffering is optional. The suffering will only last as long as you want it to. The minute you choose not to be a victim, the end of suffering is in sight. Since things are already set in motion, there is probably more pain to go through, but this will be short-lived.

I think we've all met and know people who are victims and choose to remain that way up to the end. It's so sad their lives floundered due to those personal issues having never been addressed. Our society as a whole is racked full of victims with unaddressed issues. In the process of their suffering, they cause those around them to suffer also. Their thinking goes like this: "If I'm going to suffer, then everyone else is going to suffer with me!" Thus the saying of

A Journey of Remembering

"Misery loves company."

So long as we choose to do things which are not in our own best interests, or we choose to remain a victim of some circumstance, then this is exactly what we'll have, a state of powerlessness. In a paradoxical way, it's only by accepting the fact we're powerless over things, that we will then be able to find the power to change ourselves and ultimately, our circumstances.

Where has our common sense gone? We've created a society of people who don't have to worry about a thing when making unwise choices. When a person does something that's not too smart, all they have to do is turn around and blame someone else. We've gone from having some measure of personal responsibility in our affairs to a society that preaches at us to run out and get a lawyer to make the alleged perpetrator pay handsomely. Victims won't go away, they will be heard from. We make ourselves the victims and in so doing, feel a sense of powerlessness to change our circumstances for the better.

A Journey of Remembering

CHAPTER 2: POWERLESSNESS

"A man can't pull himself off the ground by pulling on his bootstraps."
(Abraham Lincoln)

The word powerlessness has a bad time of it because it's so often misunderstood. Many people today believe the meaning to be: I'm a failure and I have no will-power, but is this what it really means? Powerlessness is actually a state of being when someone feels they're not in control of themselves or of life's situations. There is many times each and every day when every one of us lacks control over something or someone.

Let's take for instance an airplane that has lost power and is heading for a crash landing into your home. How much power do you have to control this situation? Not much. The best action to be hoped for is to run for your life. Other examples of being powerless are: mechanical things breaking with no notice, family and friends disappointing you, the kids not acting the way you want them to one-hundred percent of the time, sickness or death striking at any time, with the list going on and on. If one cannot control situations such as these, does that make one a failure? No, it just proves we're powerless to control the situation or events based solely on our own will power.

We all have times when life just happens and we're down on the mat for a ten-count. Sometimes life's challenges come more frequently or intensely to some people. For most of us, one thing is guaranteed though. We won't get through this life without these trials and tribulations. This is just part of the human condition. How we handle these situations is what determines who we really are, and in which direction we're headed. I don't care if it's loss of a job, a relationship break up, or maybe the loss of a child, whatever the circumstance, it tends to take a heavy toll on our spirits. When one of the aforementioned events happens, we have two choices. The first thing is to do nothing and just rough it out and play the victim role. The second is to attain some measure of humility, and seek an outside power (whether that's a friend, a counselor, or maybe spirituality) to help us through the difficulty.

Admitting and accepting we're powerless over something is the beginning of a delightfully new road on which to travel. It's the key to a true and newly found freedom. "How can that be?" you might ask. Before I could get anywhere with the disease of alcoholism, I had to first admit I had a problem; I had to own it in a sense. I can't let go of something I haven't first picked up. I had to accept the fact that no matter how hard I tried (self-will), I was not going to be able to drink booze like normal people. I was physically and mentally different from normal folks when it came to drinking alcohol. I couldn't control the amount I consumed, and I surely didn't know when it would end once I started.

This is a classic characteristic of any addiction - the total inability to control the outcome of the action. No amount of unaided will power can break it. It's the obsession of an insane mind. How can that be? That was my original thought also. How can I be insane? Well, a friend pointed out my insane behaviors and attitudes when it came to drinking. He pointed out the fact that I was never able to drink responsibly before, why did I think I could do so at this time? After a person pays a price for abnormal drinking and its related behaviors, the smart thing to do would be to quit, but could I? No. After many repeated failed attempts, I was beaten into submission. I couldn't control the use of alcohol in my own body, and I was rendered teachable.

What is being rendered teachable? It is being forced to see that we can no longer duck the issue of being powerless over the situation. It's at this point where the mind/ego will open to the concept that we might need some outside help, but don't expect to like it though. There hasn't been a situation yet when I've been rendered teachable that I've actually enjoyed the experience at the time of accepting it! For me, acceptance is a hard thing to deal with. I was never good at accepting anything that was less than total perfection in my mind, but as I've since found out, acceptance is the key to all my problems. *I will not find sanity or joy until I first accept the fact that everything is just the way it is supposed to be for the eventual enlightenment of my soul.* The enjoyment will come later.

Once we accept the circumstances of where we're at, then the great I AM can be toned down a bit. What's the great I AM? It's the ego, big and inflated. A big and inflated ego tells us we're okay, there's no problem here. On the other hand, an okay ego allows us to be powerless. It allows us to be less than one-hundred percent perfect people. It allows us to ask for help. Just asking for directions to the pizza parlor is an act of powerlessness and also one of great humility.

Please, don't confuse humiliation (which is feeling extreme embarrassment over something stupid we've done) with humility. Humility gets a bad rap because of its cousin's meaning. The act of being humble is simple; it's realizing and accepting the fact that *you* don't have all the answers. Saying "Please help me" is an example of being humble. Humility is seeing our self the way others see us; we're not nearly as good as we might think we are, nor as bad either. Humility is seeing our self in the proper proportion. Humbleness is a state of being you'll need to reach for if anything is to get straightened out.

We all have personality assets as well as personality debits. How do we capitalize on these assets and minimize the debits? First, we have to admit personal powerlessness. Second, we have to have some measure of humility and an open mind. Third, we have to find a power outside of ourselves that can help us. Where do we go for this outside power or help? Since the root of the problem is being powerless, we need to seek a source of power that's greater than ourself. This is where the road of enlightenment brings us to a new spirituality.

CHAPTER 3: SPIRITUALITY

Religion is for people who want to go to heaven. Spirituality is for people who've been to hell and don't want to go back.

I used to have a hard time telling the difference between religion and spirituality. In fact, I didn't know there was a difference. I always assumed they were one in the same. So, is there a difference? Yes, and I believe there's a very great one at that. Religion has always been just a few men (self-proclaimed enlightened ones) organizing other humans into a common belief system that matched their own. This common belief system is dictated from the top (where the religious leaders ply their trade) down to the common person. When you have this type of system you lose the individuality of the people in it, which is exactly what organized religion wants to accomplish. Religions have set up extremely rigid rules, dogma, and doctrine as to *how, when, where, and why* to worship God. They don't allow the individual to come to their own understanding of the Divine or Its intent for them. They've succeeded in impressing their own ideas and conceptions of God upon the masses.

If there are any free spirits in the church who don't agree with the dogma as it is set up, then things are set into motion to have them removed. They can't have free spirits running around upsetting the status quo. Every time there's a split in a religious fold, there's been a rebel not accepting what the hierarchy has put in place. These rebels have grown tired of others trying to coerce their thoughts and actions.

Religion is organized for the sole purpose of keeping the masses in check. When you have a large mass of people with the same mindset, the organization has great power. Those sitting at the top of these organizations or churches have great political power and big money figures into the equation as well. When that much political power and money are associated, there's guaranteed to be big trouble. I don't believe any religion should be set up as an organizer of spirituality. Spirituality is meant for individuals to explore themselves according to their own conceptions of God. I believe the Bible and other books were written for each individual to be used as a guide, to read and understand it as it applies to their own spiritual journey of enlightenment.

I believe Jesus came here to do away with organized religion. He showed us how to have a one-on-one relationship with the Higher Power, which doesn't include the dogma of the church. Why do you think Jesus was put to death? It was due to the fact that He was too much of a rebel for His time. In fact, Jesus is the Ultimate Rebel. Everything He stood for threatened what the church came to accept as normal religious behavior. The things people knew at the time included rigid sets of rules and conduct that had to be practiced religiously and there wasn't any room for error. The hierarchy of the church didn't want to lose their pious positions they so gloried in because they held great power over the masses. We will discuss more of this in later chapters.

As I have come to understand spirituality, it is the action of seeking a power which is greater than me on an *individual* basis; a power that can finally help me and make sense of my life. That power is God, *as I personally understand him to be.* I believe God is the last resort, not because it has to be that way, but because our egos tell us that we don't need God, and we're supposed to be self-sufficient. We try everything humanly possible first because this is the path of spiritual growth.

We try these human aids first as coping mechanisms. They may come in many forms such as drinking, drug usage, gambling, pursuit of money or power, religious fervor, relationships, love, being number one in a chosen career field, and many more forms. Anything we set up in our lives to fix us, or at least allow ourselves some time away from our darker sides, is a power greater than us. We can find solace in these pursuits for a while, but in the end the results will be the same, nil. We've been looking for a Higher Power in all the wrong places. Ultimately, these other powers can't aid us. They just *seem* to be a fix in the short term. In the end they leave us with a deeper sense of loneliness than ever before, and a hollow feeling in our hearts and souls.

I don't believe the problem lies in the *why* of our seeking of this power outside of ourselves; I believe it is in the *how* of it. We fumble around in the dark searching for who knows what, and on top of that we have no guiding light in which to help us see well. We have had no guidance in such matters. This reminds me of a saying by Sufi Rumi: *"Whoever enters the Way without a guide will take one hundred years to travel a two day journey."* And so it is. We strike off on a journey of the soul with no spiritual guidance to speak of and no idea of what or where this personal journey will take us. Our egos won't let us ask for help or directions, so instead we just wing it.

I can say from personal experience I just "winged it" for nearly thirty years and the results were nothing I could write home about. Besides, the family could have read all about it in the local newspaper anyway! I have journeyed to many places off the beaten path in search of this something which would fix me. I've been damn glad to make it out alive and in one piece, but there were times and places with which I didn't fare so well. I came back badly beaten, and scarred for life (or so I thought). It was at this point when I was rendered teachable. Finally, by being rendered teachable, I was able to accept some sort of guidance and discipline into my life, although very grudgingly at first. No longer could I do it on my own, or wing it. I badly needed help and I didn't much care where I found it, just as long as I found it.

This brings me to a story I heard once. There was this man who decided to take a walk up a mountain trail to enjoy some solitude and contemplation. He climbed a well-trodden path for some time when he decided to take a rest and enjoy the scenery. As he sat there enjoying the view, up ahead from around the bend came a mountain lion. He figured he better beat feet backwards and get to safety. Yet as he turned around to go back down the path to where he'd just come from, there stood another lion. "Now what am I going to do?" He mused to himself.

He couldn't go forward because of the menacing lion up ahead, and he couldn't retreat because the other wild beast was still there. He looked up to his left. He couldn't go up because there was nothing but a smooth rock face and no way to climb it. His gaze then shifted to the right, but that was a sheer drop off with nothing in between him and the valley floor below. "What am I going to do now?" he wondered to himself. It was just then he noticed a stout little tree sticking out below him on the cliff's face. "Strange I didn't notice it before," he thought to himself. He figured he would have to make a leap for it if there was to be any chance at all of escape from the lions that were closing in fast. He leapt and was just able to catch the tree, thus avoiding a plunge to certain death. As he hung there, amused at his sudden good fortune, his hands and arms quickly tired. Realizing he'd put himself into a worse position than before, he cried out, "Help, help me anyone!" Just then from up above came a booming voice, "Let go of the tree!" He hung there and pondered it for a second. Then he cried out even louder, "Is there anyone else up there?" You see, what the man didn't know because of the angle of the drop off, was that he was only a few feet away from a path that would lead him to safety, if only he'd let go of the tree branch.

    Let's take a few moments to analyze this story. I'm sure there've been times in all our lives where we've just been dreamily walking along just enjoying the view, when seemingly out of nowhere we find ourselves in one hell of a mess. We ask ourselves how the hell we got into it and before long we're looking for an escape. We don't even think of asking for help then. It's only after we've thrown ourselves off a cliff do we ask for help. Then when we do ask for help, we probably don't like the first reply, so we seek help from another source until we find something that suits our fancy.

    Notice though, the first time he looked off to his right, all he could see was a sheer drop off. Why didn't he notice the tree jutting out the first time? Was it there at that time? You would think he would've noticed it right away, but he didn't. I believe we get blind to such things when we're suddenly put into survival mode. Our instant reaction to a situation like this is to save ourselves by ourselves. When someone has been living a life based on self-will, the last thing to come to mind is to seek help from an outside source. Only after we've put ourselves in a worse predicament than before, do we then begin to look around for another answer to our dilemma.

Each time I've thought and pondered this story, I realize new and different things about the story itself and how it applies to situations I have in my own personal life. We all know where that booming voice came from, and I believe the God of my understanding is with us at all times. He knows when we're in trouble even before we realize it. He's already put things into motion in which we're granted an escape from the problem. I've never been in a situation yet (that jumping off place) where God had not put some sort of branch out there so I could have an escape to safety. But it would take great courage on my part to simply let go of the branch and let Him take care of the rest. Yes, I would *doubt* the advice I asked for. I wanted something I could handle or trust, something that was easy, and something that would not take too hard a shot at my pride. I had to have hard physical proof first; I wanted to see where I was going to land. The letting go of the branch required an act of courage, humility, faith, and trust on my part, and that's a tall order sometimes.

As we make a leap of faith, we badly need courage. Courage is not lack of fear; lack of fear is being brain dead. Courage is going ahead in spite of fear. Humility closely follows courage because of the simple fact it takes courage to admit we don't have all the answers and humility to ask for an outside source of help. Next is faith. Faith is a belief, trust, or reliance in something that is usually outside of us. I personally wouldn't have made it through many of the hard times without a faith and a trust that things would work out for the best in the end.

So when we make a leap of faith (or not doubting) whether with God or with something else, what we're seeking is spiritual in nature. In essence, this is the nature of the so-called "original sin" we've all heard about, when Adam and Eve first ate from the forbidden tree. The *eating* of the fruit was not the original sin (which some consider an act of defiance toward God). That was the final action based on the thought or thoughts before the action. Doubting the wisdom of God surely appeared before the defiant act of eating the forbidden fruit.

Let's look at the very first words uttered in the Bible by the serpent. They were: "Did God really say, 'You must not eat from any tree in the garden?'" Doubt was instilled in the mind of humans for the very first time, and so began the process of doubting God by not asking, "Why not eat the fruit from the tree that's in the middle of the garden, what's it going to hurt?" This is doubt, pure and simple; followed by an act of laziness on their part as they didn't put forth the effort to question God about it.

I believe this is what God sent his Son to do on this earthly realm; to remove all doubt. The life he lived and the miracles he performed is the result of having no doubt in the power of God. He wiped out the so-called original sin. He proved what could happen to one's own life if there is no doubt in the power of God. Jesus remembered where he came from and never truly left.

So just as with the man on the mountain path, or with Adam and Eve, when in times of stress, they doubted their own knowledge of the situation. They doubted their own faith, and they doubted their own experiences up to that time. We all begin to look elsewhere because we have doubts about the things we've been taught or have come to accept as truth from someone else. We begin to look outside of ourselves for answers and guidance. I believe this is all part of the spiritual process of removing doubt, thus getting to know ourselves, and in turn getting to know the Divine.

A Journey of Remembering

CHAPTER 4: CONCEPTIONS OF GOD

Well people don't need doctors.

Getting to know the Divine (or Higher Power, or God, or whatever you understand Him or Her to be) is a process of remembering; we'll talk more about this in later chapters. Steady progress is what we strive for. In the process of getting a new understanding of a Higher Power, we must now look at what our present conception of Him is. Does the conception you have of Him work for you today? Is He a comfort for you? Can you look to Him/Her for support in times of trouble or strife? Are you afraid of Him? Do you trust Him? Do you love Her? Is He your friend? Do you even believe She exists?

I think these are some of the questions we must ask ourselves to determine where we're presently at. After asking ourselves these questions, we may need to let go of some of these conceptions of God we've been taught, simply because they no longer serve our needs. We need to get some different ideas that will work for us. We should try to practice an open mind in this area. It won't take too long to see if the God you presently understand is working for you.

The God of my understanding as I was growing up was a God I was taught to fear. And I mean **FEAR**! He was just waiting for me to step out of line and then He would let the hammer fall, and fall hard. I was taught I would be severely punished for any misstep I took. It would be just like in Noah's day when the people were not acting the way God wanted them to, and He made it rain for forty days and nights and killed them all. That's the type of God I was taught to worship.

Thinking about it now, who in their right mind would want to have a relationship with something like that? I sure didn't and don't to

A Journey of Remembering

this day. I want something guiding my will and life to be something I can respect, love, admire, and have as a friend; something that's there to help me when I'm down; not kick me, nor ridicule me, nor try to do me in. I want something that has compassion for me when I'm not whole, nor a saint. What I needed to do was let go of some old ideas which had become ingrained in me while at the same time pick up some fresh new ideas which would work from here on out. Here's a little observation I've been able to make over the years: You will not let go of an old idea until you are ready to embrace a new one; it's that simple. It's impossible to hang onto both ideas at the same time.

This is the beginning of our search for a new spiritual lifestyle while seeking a new understanding of this Power. We have to have a willingness to let go of these ideas that haven't worked for us and at that same time, have a willingness to seek out new ideas that *will* work for us. Where do we find these fresh ideas? I believe we need to look to the people for whom these new ideas are working. A good source for this might be your local bookstore or a spiritual group of like-minded people.

Take a little time to go and explore a bookstore. Just keep an open mind and see what strikes your fancy. If something does strike, then you're supposed to read it. Read about or talk to people who've been through real hardships in their personal lives. It will work much better to find people who have situations like your own. Find the commonness that you share with them. Reach out and become a *part of* something, not *apart from* things.

Your new understanding will most likely come through other people. I personally have come to the conception of a Higher Power that works for me from little tidbits of other people's conceptions. I no longer believe God to be punishing no matter what I do or don't do. I no longer believe God to be something that doesn't care for me. I also don't believe God is out to destroy me if I don't do just as He wants me to. I no longer believe in a burning Hell where we're sent because we're bad or we can't adjust our actions to fit the mold of "righteous" people.

Here are some more of my new conceptions or understandings of God today: He's a very loving God, just as a parent would love a

A Journey of Remembering

child. He wants what's best for me, whatever that may be. He hurts when He sees me struggling to find my way. He shares my joy when I'm happy. He wants me to be the very best that I can be in whatever I choose to be. He loves to be included in my life. He has a purpose in His life too. He doesn't take joy in seeing sickness and death in something He created. He loves to be a part *of* me, not apart *from* me. He loves for me to grow and thrive, to be happy and free.

I think we need to look at ourselves while forming a new understanding of God. Let's use a little common sense here. Are we not created in God's image? As a parent of seven children, I see it through a parent's eyes first. I dearly love all my children; I only want what is best for them. I try to share my experiences and wisdom with them to the best of my ability. I don't want them to hurt emotionally (or physically for that matter), but as any parent knows, there's going to be hurt and pain in their lives. That's just the way it is. Let me use this example: You teach a child the stove is hot. The child can be hurt severely if it touches the hot stove. We watch over them as best we can so they don't get hurt, but the day comes when the child touches the hot stove.

The reality of this situation is that we can't dedicate our whole life to watching the child so they never touch the hot stove again, or to protect them from themselves. They have to learn the hard way not to touch the hot stove, and that experience is painful for them and for us. It's no fun to watch a child be hurt, either physically or emotionally, and I believe this is what God goes through. He hurts when He sees us going through these learning experiences.

And so as a parent, God watches and lets us experience what we need to experience so we may remember. Part of being a good parent is being there for the children when they're having a growth experience, while letting them know it's okay to go through this stuff and we're not judging them. We let them know we still love and accept them no matter what the outcome is.

I've also come to the conclusion that God loves to have a friendly relationship with each and every one of us on an individual basis. What is a friend to me? A friend is someone I can trust wholeheartedly and will listen without condemnation. A friend loves me in spite of my shortcomings and is also someone I can depend on, and they in turn can depend on me. A friend is someone I can share my deepest secrets with, and also my greatest hopes and dreams - someone I can just "be" with. There are no conditions, laws, or expectations. A friend is just someone to have fun with. Now there's a mind bender! A God you can have fun with which is encased in a relationship of unconditional love. Now wouldn't that be a cool God?

In gaining a new understanding of this Higher Power in our lives, we need to turn our lives over to Him so He can guide us. We should be able to plainly see where self-will has gotten many of us. We've hit our problems from every angle with self-will. It just hasn't worked well at all. In turning our lives over to a God we can understand, we also turn our self-will over. We allow Life to mold us in the way that is best, just as a parent would.

Our fears will kick in strong at this juncture, because the ego begins to fear for itself. What will become of *me* if I turn my will over to God? Am I going to be some religious freak? Absolutely not! The only thing people around you will notice is a new sense of serenity and peace. They'll know your life has changed, but won't really be able to put a finger on how you did it. God doesn't need a grand show to demonstrate His abilities!

I personally believed I had to stop doing all the things I thought were wrong in order for God to accept me. I thought I had to be perfect. For instance, I believed I must quit smoking, get my haircut, lose my earrings, have my tattoos removed, and clean up my language, but you see, this is who I really am. God wants us just the way we are. *Well people don't need doctors.*

CHAPTER 5: THE GREATER PLAN

We are all spirit creatures experiencing apartness from God and then ultimately, reunion with God.

No matter where one goes on this earth, no matter the nationality, tribe, color of skin, or language spoken, all people have a concept of something greater than themselves. They all try to make sense of why they're here, where they came from, and where they're going after their life is concluded. They may try to deny that part of themselves for however long, but in the end they're still faced with these nagging questions. I don't believe any human being who hasn't embraced their journey of enlightenment, and is facing imminent death, can't help but ask "What's this all for? What's this all about?"

I believe this is why we're here on planet earth in human flesh. It is while on this physical plane that we experience things that can't be experienced on the other side. I also believe this is all part of a greater plan. We were always spiritual (or Spirit) and always will be; having this present life experience is just part of the process. What might be a reason for taking on human form? How about experiencing God and ourselves? Knowing who God and who we are is just that, knowing; it's not the highest level. Experiencing and feeling is the ultimate level. There's a big difference between *knowing* something and *feeling* something!

Take an example like this: A person has a desire to be a doctor and they have excelled in school and moved up the ladder. They go on to college and then on to medical school. After they finish all the testing and internships, they're presented a license to practice medicine. This only proves they have the required *knowledge* to be a doctor of medicine, but they haven't really *experienced* being a doctor.

All the decisions made as an intern were watched over and guided. Any procedure done for a patient was carefully reviewed by other more knowledgeable doctors (teachers).

I don't doubt they have a sense of what it is to be a doctor, but it's not the same as when they're personally responsible for the life and death decisions they make day-in and day-out. Sensing something and experiencing something are two different things. Ask any doctor who's been in practice for a while, and I'm convinced he/she could tell you what the experience is really like. I'm quite sure it will be a whole lot different compared to their residency. That goes with anything we do - no matter the occupation, social status, political view, wages we earn, or our degree of spirituality; knowing something is much different than actually experiencing it.

We all have an idea of what it is to be rich in the monetary sense. We see rich people all the time on television, in magazines, and on the streets. We see what they buy, and how they use or misuse their money. We possess the knowledge of what rich people are. We've gained a sense of being rich, but the experience of being rich is a whole different story. Very few people indeed have that actual experience. When we know something, that is knowledge, but when we experience and feel something, then it's Divine. Why is it Divine? Because when we experience being something, so does God. That's part of the Divine Plan. Once we've experienced something, we've lived it. Once we've lived it, then we own it. You can honestly say then, "I've been there, done that! I've bought the hat, T-shirt, and the coffee cup."

So now let's get back to the Greater Plan. Think about these questions for a minute. How can you experience darkness if all you've ever experienced is light? How can you experience joy if you've never experienced sadness? How can you experience trust if all you have ever known was fear? How can you experience God if you've always felt apart from God?

When you were with God, you *knew* perfection; you just couldn't experience it because you didn't have the opposite, imperfection. You can only get that experience here in physical form because in the spirit form you can't be anything but pure love. Love knows nothing of fear, distrust, hurt, frustration, loneliness, depression, and the other negative human emotions we have here. None of us truly knew what imperfection was because we hadn't experienced it; it was just a mental concept, something for us to ponder. So with God's help we took on human form to experience imperfection (or lack of love) so in turn we can truly experience perfection and love unconditionally; to re-member.

So now when you read or remember the story of Adam and Eve and the original sin, you can see it in a different light. Yes, when we were in the so-called Garden of Eden, we had perfection; we just didn't know it! We couldn't experience it or truly appreciate it until we didn't have it anymore, and so we took our physical selves out of the garden to truly know and experience God in all his glory. God gave us free will to do whatever we needed to do to experience life and for the evolution of our souls. I believe we *gladly* ate from the tree of knowledge of good and bad, and with God's blessing I might add! How else could we know and experience, and thus in turn evolve? Maybe we should be calling it the "original blessing" instead!

I believe this was just the beginning of God's great Master Plan for us. Part of the deal for coming to this realm was we would consciously forget where we came from. Otherwise, we couldn't truly experience "apartness" from God, but we would retain at a deep subconscious level the knowledge of where we came from and where we would return at a later time. It's the yearning of the mind that cries out to God, because the soul is never lost; the soul never forgets. The soul is on a mission, and it will forever seek to fulfill that mission. It may take hundreds of lifetimes on this earth, but what the hell, we live forever anyway. We've got all the time in the universe at our disposal.

What you're here to experience this time through is part of your own individual spiritual journey; I can't say what yours is. I had a hard time trying to define my own, let alone anyone else's. I ask you to keep an open mind about the following: What if we're really spirit creatures and we choose to take on human form in this physical plane? Let's say one day we get together with some fellow souls and begin discussing how we'd like to improve our soul's evolution through another lifetime here on earth. Of course we need to pick some sort of

A Journey of Remembering

life experience that helps us to advance to a higher spiritual level, as there is no such thing as regression in the spiritual sense.

We need the help of these fellow spirit creatures who also have an agenda for their own evolutionary needs. So we make an agreement that at the appointed time we'll make our entrance into the world and begin our journey with them. Let's say we need to learn more about the proper use of power, so we pick a family to be born into which has much political power. Living this life, we gain another experience with a different viewpoint from previous lifetimes. Can you imagine how many lifetimes it would take to achieve a well-balanced perception of human emotions and life experiences? It boggles the mind to even try to comprehend it. I believe each and every one of our goals is to advance, not hinder the growth of all humanity through our own personal journeys.

Can anyone find me a better answer as to why certain people are just attracted to certain positions in life? Why aren't we all ditch diggers? Why aren't we all auto mechanics? Why do certain people go on to be in the clergy? Why do people have "natural gifts" in one area or another? Is it all because of genetics where some people are born with a special natural gift gene? Why are some people happy with a simple life and yet we find others who are always grabbing for more?

I believe everyone in our lives is here for a purpose. That purpose being to help us grow in whatever area we need to expand in. I also believe every physical thing in our lives serves that purpose as well. I don't care if it's a particular job, car, financial situation, physical ailment, or family member; it's there for the soul's evolution, and when that purpose has been served it's removed. In this way, all material things are a means to an end, not end means as they are conceived of today.

Now you may need a certain thing in your life for only a day or maybe a lifetime, however long doesn't matter. What matters is the purpose of these tools as they serve you. Why as human beings do we choose certain people to be partnered with? Why are they sometimes referred to as our "soul mates"? Of all the people on this earth, why do we pick the ones we do? Is it all chance, coincidence, or maybe just dumb luck?

When we get into the spiritual plane more, you'll be able to see there's no such thing as coincidence or accidents, and there's surely nothing such as dumb luck. *Everything has a purpose!* In God's Master Plan there can be nothing but perfection. Everything that happens is to advance the human soul individually, and in the end advance humanity as a whole. If everything that happens to us is left to chance or luck, there will be no human species because we would've self-destructed long ago. There's no way we could have ever become a society of peoples.

Even the atoms we're made of have a purpose, a definite path they're on. Each one has a specific job to do. You can't make a proton do the job of a neutron; they have their purpose in life. They are all guided by some unseen force to do the job they do. Why as humans, can't we accept the fact we all have a specified job to do and do it in harmony with our fellows? It's the path we chose long ago and yet we fight it all the way to the gates of death. Why can't we accept the fact there's a Guiding Force out there to help us experience whatever we've come here to experience?

CHAPTER 6: ALLOWING GOD IN THE DOOR.

"As we sow, so shall we reap." (Psalms 46:10)

We can't, or won't accept the fact that God *belongs* in our journey of enlightenment because of our over-inflated egos. Man, through his so-called great knowledge and intelligence, has developed a characteristic he believes is a great asset, and that's being self-sufficient. Man believes science can cure all things that ail us. We've reached a point where we believe all we have to do is swallow a little pill and all our emotional and mental maladies are taken care of. Why feel emotional pain or even a little discomfort when we can pop a pill and watch it vanish? We've become experts in the ability to repair the human body so we may live longer and longer, and yet our society as a whole has become more discontented and dysfunctional. We've become disillusioned with the sciences as a whole because in the end, they can't fix what's wrong with us. We're beginning to see we can't do it with our own resources; we desperately need an outside source of help.

I take my hat off to M. Scott Peck, M.D. (author of *The Road Less Traveled* and many other books) for realizing this lack of spiritual guidance in the sciences of today. He's on the cutting edge of merging the two, and I believe he's experiencing some success in this area. His books have been at the top of the bestseller lists many times. Millions of people have been reading his books because they're not satisfied with the status quo. They all know they need to advance their thinking because pill-popping short cuts aren't proving to be the great panacea they are sold as. These pills will never give the results that are necessary to grow into more enlightened human beings.

What we need to see is the knowledge we've gained as human beings is to be used in *conjunction* with our already established spiritual tools on this journey of enlightenment. We've set up knowledge in the physical sense as the end means, the ultimate in fixing ourselves, when it should be used as a means to an end. My advice is to use counseling or psychiatric help in a way that will enhance our spiritual condition, not take away from it. Let's use modern scientific means to not only make our lives more comfortable and bearable, but to ultimately lead us to a new type of spirituality in comfortable circumstances. Let's use our science of astronomy to see not just how this was all created, but for what purpose; the why of it. God could've made the heavens consist of only our little galaxy called the Milky Way. He didn't need to make all this other stuff just for us to look at one day. There was a purpose behind it all. What is it?

Whenever I have a question of importance, I try to seek out answers from someone who is knowledgeable about the subject. Would it be wrong then to go right to the source when we have questions of the spirit? What's wrong with going straight to God and asking Him to help solve a riddle or maybe a problem we might have? Personally I was always afraid of that. I always thought only someone of good moral character could do that.

Please believe me when I say I didn't think I was good enough for God. I believed God didn't want to have anything to do with people like me. Not only was I of questionable moral fabric, at times I could see downright evil in some of things I thought and did. As a matter of fact I thought, "Why *would* He want to have anything to do with me?" (Some more old ideas I would have to let go of). Anyway, I was taught while first forming a relationship with God, I needed to be honest with Him. He needed to hear from the real Nathan, not the one I always pretended to be. Now there's an eye opener! I was shocked at this new idea. I would put on this act of who I thought He wanted me to be. Little did I know that He was seeing right through my charade the whole time.

I never really prayed to God much before. The times I did pray, I found myself hanging over a toilet bowl puking my guts out from another drunk gone bad. I would beseech Him out loud, "God, please get me out of this one and I'll never do it again!" That was my prayer at the time. God, I used to get sick, so sick I just wanted to die. Well, guess what? He kept up his end of the deal and saw me through it, yet I didn't keep up my end of the bargain for many years to come. Yet each time it would happen, I would find myself saying the same prayer over and over again.

There were other occasions when I prayed to him too. These were always a result of another self-imposed crisis I managed to put myself into. Whether it had to do with the law, my wife, my children, or my behaviors, it didn't matter, the prayer was the same: "God get me out of this one and I won't ever do it again!" God had become a pinch hitter for me. I only wanted Him in my life when I had nowhere else to turn. I only wanted Him when things were looking very bad for me.

You see, I harbored resentment toward God in these areas because the same things kept happening over and over again. He didn't change me a bit and He didn't change my circumstances either. I finally came to the realization that if things were to change, I would have to lead the battle and take responsibility for my own actions and feelings. I would also have to come to a *new* understanding of this Higher Power. I would have to gain a new way of seeing Him. Since honesty is the best policy, that's what I did - I got real honest with Him.

He got to see me for just who I was. He saw the very angry and hurt Nathan. If things had not gone just the way I thought they should, I'd curse Him out with every foul word I knew, and that's quite a substantial list. If I were hurt, I'd scream at Him and ask Him why He was doing this to me. Thankfully I only did this when I was alone, or else someone who was watching me would've thought I'd lost it, and in a sense I had. I finally overcame the desire to hide from Him. If He wanted me, He was going to see and hear it all!

That was the way I learned how to pray differently. I needed to pray honestly. We need to say to God if we're mad at him: "God I'm pissed at you" or if we're disappointed in things, we need to say, "God I'm really disappointed in this or that." Don't forget too, when things are going okay, to let Him know that also. There's nothing wrong with a "Thank you" or "Way to go God, we're doing okay" now and then. The greatest prayers to say though are ones of gratitude. I don't think you should forget about the other great prayers or the ones in the Good Book (Bible) because they have their place.

I believe He wants to have a one-on-one relationship with each and every one of us that includes the good, the bad, and the ugly. You see, since He's ultimate love, He understands. He knows we're an emotional lot and we just act like two-year-olds sometimes; He doesn't take it personally though. He loves us for just who we are and he loves us in spite of ourselves (another definition of unconditional love).

This coming to know or understand the Higher Power is a journey that can involve some time though. It's not usually something that's going to happen overnight, though it truly can happen in a manner of seconds if you embrace it. I spent many years running away from God and I figured it was going to take a few years to get back to Him. Once you've gained guidance in your life as to these matters, the journey doesn't have to take so long. The journey will go as fast as you're able to go. You'll really need to keep an open mind about spiritual concepts because the old ideas won't leave just like that. A heads-up here; you're sure to get some flak from those close to you because they don't or won't understand what you're doing. They may be impressed with the results, but chances are they won't approve of the path you've chosen to get there because this path requires major changes in the way you think and act.

Whenever there's major change involved, people don't necessarily like it. You may have to let go of family traditions, the religion you were raised in, or maybe some of the crowd you've been hanging around with. This will require some personal fortitude (self-will put to good use) to stick with what you feel is right even though it may be against the seeming forces that surround you. Don't forget, we're all on our own personal journeys; we must travel the road as we see fit. The more we're able to allow those around us to be where they're at, the more they'll allow us to go down the road we must travel. This is a spiritual law; whatever goes around, comes around. We'll discuss this in much greater detail in the chapters to come.

A Journey of Remembering

CHAPTER 7: DEFINING WHO WE ARE

You can't get to where you want to go if you don't know where you're at.

Part of the process of getting to know and experience a new Power in your life is the need to examine your own life, because as with any relationship, it's a two-way street. Both parties need to contribute to it. No relationship is worthwhile if it's one-sided, so you need to define who you are at the present time. That's the easy part. Who you see yourself as is easily defined within a few minutes by grabbing a piece of paper and a pencil and writing it down. On the paper you will need to make six columns. The column heads should be titled: *My Morals, My Resentments, My Fears, My Weaknesses, My Strengths, My Hopes, and My Dreams.*

First off, I ask you to be *totally* honest here, no fibbing or half-truths because the whole course of your spiritual journey will depend upon it. You're now engaged in the process of creating a new life. This new life must be based on firm groundwork. I can't stress enough how important this work is. I know for a fact one's spiritual rewards are directly proportional to the amount of effort and honesty one puts into the process. So again, I ask you to please be diligent and trust the process.

What's the purpose behind these lists? Very simply, you need to define who you really are, and in defining that, you'll find out what makes you tick. How you think and act (or your character) is determined by the sum of your whole life's experience up to this very moment. Everything you've ever thought, seen, or felt has had an impact on who you are today. Some of these things may have very minor impacts, while others may be very large indeed. Another very important reason you need to do this footwork is it's part of the process of *ex-pressing* (or pushing out from within you) who you really are (those areas of your personality that you'd just as soon keep hidden), not the stage character you present to everyone else.

We all have a darker side of us we would prefer to never be seen by others because if this side of us were to shine through, we fear those around us might not like what they see. With them seeing us for who we really are, we fear their rejection and the certain pain that's to follow. I've seen many people go to great lengths to keep the "off color" side of them hidden, with myself leading the list. Why did I go to such great lengths to keep certain things hidden? It was fear, pure and simple. Fear I may be rejected for the things I thought, fear of other people thinking I'm stupid or something, and fear they may see the real Nathan (whom I thought was of highly questionable moral fiber).

When a person has fears that were as large as mine, they do some really irrational and insane things to keep them secret. I can remember having so many secrets about myself and the things that went on in my life that I would live in total fear and dread of the day anyone would find out about them. I'm here to tell you those secrets and those "tales of the dark side" can and will kill. They'll kill any relationship you're currently in, or will be in down the road. They'll kill your very will to live, and they'll kill off any chance of obtaining that vitally needed Power to fix things. In the end, those secrets will kill you!

Why do you think so many people have turned to drugs, drinking, gambling, over-eating, and various other forms of denial which allow them to forget those very secrets, those areas of their dark side they'd just as soon stay buried? If there's to be any hope of success in your journey of enlightenment, these areas have to come to light. Sounds like a tall order to fill, huh? Yes and no. While doing these lists, you'll be able to see patterns that have been detrimental to your soul's journey, and before you're even done with the process, you *will* have discovered a gold mine of sorts! So let's get on with these lists and see how much we can find out about ourselves. Let's make it an adventure, so to speak. I wouldn't ask you to do anything I haven't personally done before. I have made lists such as these on quite a few occasions. Before you grab a piece of paper and start the following lists, let me help define these areas for you. Let's start off with morals.

Morals:

We define our own personal set of morals by our own life's experiences. By the way, what are morals and how did you get them? First off, let's use a simple definition of morals. Morals are a set of beliefs that define common acceptable behavior. In a sense it's a code of conduct. Much of our moral code is dictated by laws the government has set up and also by what religion deems necessary to enforce their set of rules. For instance, it's illegal to cheat on your taxes, it's illegal to steal, it's illegal to take another's life, it's illegal to speed on the highway, etc. The same laws governing daily behavior for many of us may also be classified as "moral" by the church.

I believe we all consider it immoral to take another's life, and the same can be said with stealing, but do you consider it immoral to say "Screw the speed limit" when rushing a baby to the hospital because of an accident or sickness? Or, do you consider it immoral to take another human life in defense of our own, whether in your own home or as an act of war? What about the morality of keeping a hundred dollar bill that's just fallen from someone's pocket in the checkout line? This is why it's so difficult for government and religion to legislate morality to the masses.

There really are no hard and fast rules about anything. I will repeat that, *there are no hard and fast rules about anything*. It's our perspective of the situation that makes things so-called "right" or "wrong." It's a terrible tragedy when someone dies in a car accident, yet the owner of a funeral home makes his living from people dying. The auto body repairperson makes his living repairing smashed cars. As you can see, it all depends on your perspective of things as to whether something is a tragedy or a God-send.

There is a lot of grey area in these types of situations. There doesn't have to be a law against something to make it immoral. The same thing applies for being moral; there's no law that says we have to be friendly to our neighbors, but the morally good thing to do is to be friendly and loving. So as you can see, defining a new set of morals is something like a journey into the unknown. You may have a basic blueprint of sorts, but it also leaves a whole lot of wiggle room in which to define your own set of morals.

In defining my own set of morals, I needed to look at them first. I needed to write them down to see what I believed to be true or okay for me. Back when, these were some of the things I believed to be immoral: divorce (except in the instance of adultery), murder, theft, lying, cheating, rape, assault, homosexuality, gambling, abortion, the use of tobacco, and a few others. This is a good list that closely resembles most religions of yesterday and today, but over the years I didn't seem to be able to maintain these codes of conduct.

The more I failed to uphold these preset morals I was taught, the more I saw myself as a failure, and this is where my problems began. These were somebody else's morals that were impressed upon me. They were a set of morals *someone else* thought I should live by. In examining my own set of morals, I found some that would work for me and some that needed to be tuned up a bit. I needed a new set that would work for me personally, a set I could live with.

I was able to design a new set by looking back on my life and seeing what worked for me and what didn't. I also reflected on how I felt about some of the morals I was taught. For instance, I asked myself about homosexuality and what I felt about it. Were these people really *that* bad? I've had the opportunity to know a few gay men and women, and I couldn't for the life of me see anything wrong with them. Yes, they had a different sexual preference than I, but they still told good jokes, they still loved their families (in spite of their families telling them to go to hell), they went out and worked, earned a paycheck, and they loved to be loved, just like the rest of us. After appraising the situation a bit, I concluded they weren't any worse than me, maybe even better. Who was I to point a finger? I figure being an alcoholic isn't far from being gay when it comes to what society and religions think of your moral character.

A Journey of Remembering

I have another personal example for you to think about. As I was being brought up as a child, the rule for marriage was that it was not over "until death do you part." Short of proving adultery, the church I belonged to would not recognize the divorce and the divorcing party would then be ex-communicated if they were ever to remarry, because the party that remarried would then commit the act of adultery. But what if just too much damage was done to the marriage union and it couldn't be repaired? Being an alcoholic, I caused extensive damage to my first marriage that could not be repaired.

There were also some issues within the union I needed to address, the main one being that I was married within months of graduating high school. You see, no matter what I did, I knew I could somehow talk my wife into taking me back, being totally sincere at the time in regard to changing my attitude and behavior. God knows I wanted to change, because I couldn't keep living like I was which resulted in hurting the family tremendously. After realizing I couldn't seem to change things with my very best will power, the best option for all concerned was to get out.

Since there was so much damage done and I couldn't see any way of it working out, I considered a divorce, but when I'd think of that, the moral code that was ingrained in me by the church and my parents would soon haunt me. I would think to myself, "Just because I have some personal issues to work on, it's no reason to get a divorce. Besides, if I did get a divorce I would be severely punished by God." What a way to live! The way I saw it, I was screwed no matter what I did.

So part of my own spiritual development was to divorce, and in a sense "burn that bridge." I couldn't just scorch the paint; it needed to be totally burnt to ashes. It wasn't an easy thing to do; in fact it was one of the hardest things I've done in my whole life. Here I was, a man walking out on his wife and four children. I felt like a total failure as a husband and a father, but for all concerned it was for the best. I don't recommend divorce as an easy out. It's not to be taken lightly, because it's the fall of a family unit.

Another reason divorce shouldn't be entered into lightly is the reason(s) the marriage didn't work out in the first place. If you don't know why it failed, then the mistakes will be repeated, and the result will be the same. After assessing the situation and seeing that the relationship itself is coming in between yourself and the Higher Power, then you have a hard choice to make. You need to be ready to go to any lengths to obtain this new spiritual relationship with God. Remember the story of the mountain trail? You may have to make a leap for it. Now let's move onto the next item on the list.

Resentments:

Alex Witchel of the New York Times once said: *"Resentment is like taking poison and waiting for the other person to die."* No truer statement about what resentment is has ever been said. Holding onto resentments will rot you from the inside out. Not only does it do damage on the inside, it also cuts you off from the spiritual sustenance of your Higher Power. When harboring resentment you become your own Higher Power. By holding on to these resentments, you rehash the episode over and over again in your mind. You keep giving it life by the energy of thinking about it all the time. *It won't die because you won't let it die.* How do you get resentments? Resentment comes through the action of pushing your own moral code on to someone else, the same as was done to you. You believe they should act in a certain manner, and when they don't, you get angry and form resentment toward them.

We can also push our own moral code onto institutions, governments, societies, and religions, and when they fail to live up to these personal codes of conduct we form more resentment. We coddle and caress them as if they were a pet of ours. It's no wonder where the saying of having a pet peeve comes from! By keeping these resentments a pet, we embellish ourselves and feel righteous and strong. We set ourselves up as being better than those the resentment is against. In again comes the great I AM. Here's the boisterous ego raising its ugly head once more.

Resentment will show itself as hatred and disgust. These are both emotional booby traps. Each time we bring up these resentments in our mind, we re-live the trauma or supposed trauma. These will

A Journey of Remembering

bring back feelings of anger, hatred, and retaliation because they lie just below the surface of our consciousness if left untreated. They'll impact your life in many absurd ways. They'll show up in decisions you make or fail to make. No decision based on that much anger or hatred is good for any of the parties involved.

Resentments may come in many forms. You may not even be aware of the resentment at all. Your ego may have very cleverly hidden it from you through the guise of self-justification or rationalization. What is self-justification? Self-justification is when you go about making it okay in your mind for some behavior or attitude to live on in you, even though you know in your hearts-of-hearts what you're doing is just putting something or someone else down so as to elevate yourself above them.

Here's a good example of self-justification from my personal files: After being gone most of the weekend partying with friends and neglecting the family once again, my wife would confront me about my behavior. I would tell her I *deserved* a little free time because I worked my ass off all week providing for the family and I deserved to let my hair down. Self-justification comes in because I resented someone else telling me what to do, or because she was trying to impress her own moral code on me. In essence, what I was trying to do was make it okay, and to make me right and her wrong. Simply put, I was trying to justify a selfish behavior. I broke my own moral code and had to somehow justify it in my own mind.

Rationalization on the other hand is making up an excuse for some selfish behavior we're about to do or have done. An example: I wouldn't have to rob the bank if I still had my job. What I'm trying to do is to make the "not okay" behavior look okay because I wouldn't take responsibility for myself and go get another job like normal people do. With rationalization, we make it an art form of blaming outside circumstances for our own selfish behaviors.

As in a mathematical problem, we can check to see if a theory is correct by just reversing the order of the problem. As in one + two = three, we can take three - two = one. Self-justification plus rationalization will equal resentment. And reversing the order, take resentment and minus self-justification and you will find rationalization. Or you can minus rationalization from resentment and find self-justification standing alone.

How do we overcome resentment? First off, it helps to say a prayer for the person or thing and ask God to bless them. Do this daily for as long as it takes. It usually won't take more than a week or two. Another helpful thing I've found that works is to allow them to have their own set of morals. Quit pushing your moral code onto others. They're on their own spiritual journey. *Let it be!*

Another way to be rid of resentment is to walk a day in their shoes. Three-quarters of the reason for getting resentment is we don't understand where they're coming from. It's *only* through true understanding from which true forgiveness can come. A guidepost that the resentment is gone is that you'll now be able to see the good in the situation, and no longer have to worry about it or waste mind time on it because it won't affect you anymore. Now on to the list of fears, it's a big one.

Fear:

We can all probably define fear pretty simply. It's an apprehension of imminent danger or lack of control over future events. We don't ever have fear over past events because they can no longer harm us, even though we may be fearful of the consequences of those past events. The actual past event can't harm us, so there is no fear. These fears may be of the physical sense (as in physical harm) or they may be of the emotional variety. I think we need to deal with the emotional fears we all have, as they're much more important in the way we live our lives today. Emotional fear is an underlying thread that weaves its ugly way through our very being and moral fabric. We all act the way we do because of these fears. Let's make a short list of the more common types of emotional fear.

Fear of not being accepted.
Fear of not being loved.
Fear of losing someone or something.
Fear of losing our livelihood.

Fear of being sick or incapacitated.
Fear of not being good enough.
Fear of being misunderstood.
Fear of God's wrath.
Fear of dying.
Fear of not having enough.
Fear of misunderstood intentions.
Fear of rejection.

This list could go on for many pages (at least it did in mine), but I think you get the drift of things. Add to the list as you see fit. If one were to put a little effort into it, one can see where we all have these fears (whether big or small) and digging a little deeper, we'll be able to see how they've affected our every thought and action. Notice though that all these fears are based on an imminent or future event; not one has to deal with past events. Again, past events carry no fear. Do you know what the four letters of fear stand for? "**F**" is for future, "**E**" is for events, "**A**" is for aren't, and "**R**" is for real. In short, **F**uture **E**vents **A**ren't **R**eal.

We can experience apprehension about future events. This could turn into a full-blown phobia of sorts if we dwell on them too much. We may begin to do all sorts of stupid things that aren't good for us, so as to avoid a "possibility." What might some of these possibilities be? We may have to be in a wheelchair and have someone care for us (this will hurt our pride). We may lose our coveted job and then we have to start at the bottom (again our pride is hurt). We may have to let go of someone we deeply love (again, hurt pride plus loss of companionship).

Have you noticed a little pattern developing here? Underlying all these fears and those we can add to the list is our pride (ego) and the damage to it in some way or another. The ego is scared and so in turn makes the mind scared, which results in this emotion of fear. It's the great I AM shouting again. For me, fear ruled my life in all areas. I would go far out of my way not to hurt someone's feelings, but in the process of doing this, I would deny myself. I would place their emotional well-being on myself and make it my job for them to be happy again.

What I just described was being a people pleaser. I wanted everyone not only to like Nathan, but to really love him. I would go the extra mile to do things that helped you, but during the process of this, I denied myself and my loved ones of those very same things. Pride played a big role too. Pride allowed me to stand back and say, "Look at what I did for you." Needless to say, this was a very selfish behavior on my part when done for that reason.

The pattern that has developed here is finding pride right behind every fear. The same pattern will develop if you were to make a list for your prideful self. Close behind pride, you'll find a fear or fears in there somewhere. Don't be too hasty to discount this pattern, as fear and pride make up the cutting sides of a double-edged sword. Pride says you don't have to look at these areas because there isn't anything wrong, while fear says you dare not look because you may not be able to handle what you find; it's that simple.

Weaknesses:

We can all see when using a search light over our lives, where the areas are that need attention. Maybe we've been able to see and work on them ourselves, or perhaps a few people have pointed some things out. Before we take any more action on these weaknesses, we need to identify them first. These weaknesses will all be *symptoms* of something deeper in our character. Let's take a short look at some possible weaknesses we might possibly have.

How about always being late to appointments or engagements? We've all heard that it's "fashionable to be late." The symptom here is being late. Is our schedule so full that we can't make it to a function on time? What's the underlying cause here? I believe it is pride. Pride likes to make a big show of things. Doesn't using the word "fashionable" give it the connotation of being glitzy and a little prideful? I take it to mean: "Hey everyone, look at me. I'm important!" Believe it or not, Adolph Hitler used this very method on purpose; by keeping the crowds waiting (sometimes for up to an hour) he felt they would believe what he was going to say was very important.

A Journey of Remembering

The next time you're in a situation where there's a room full of people and the meeting is about to begin, glance over your shoulder and take a peek at the latecomers. Oh, you'll see the disheveled ones hurrying in and finding a place to sit down, but keep watching. Usually after the meeting has begun, there'll be one who has the natural ability of making everyone in the place turn around and notice them. They'll also have a strut that broadcasts, "I'm important." Lastly, they'll usually try to find a seat up front so they can make the grand entrance complete.

Another weakness to possibly look at is being gullible or being a pushover. These are only the symptoms of the weakness. What's the underlying cause for this behavior? It is being less assertive than one should be. This usually comes from being put down during the formative childhood years, and will continue into adulthood. After being told you are less-than, you turn into a people pleaser in order to win approval. You try to be the perfect person, or at least what you perceive to be perfect.

Another weakness we may have on the list could be a lack of trust. This comes from an episode or many episodes in which we trusted someone or something and were badly burned in the process. Being able to trust again has been a process of elimination for me. Those of you who don't naturally trust most people right off the bat will have a tough time in learning to trust again. I've found through the process of trusting people again that you can get burned a time or two. As with any lesson, you become a little more cynical when the next one comes along. Being cynical, you don't put as much on the line next time, just in case you have good reason not to trust them in the first place. But with effort and a little time, one can learn to trust again.

I just used these examples as an illustration of the kind of searching one has to do to get to the root cause of the behaviors. Remember, there can be no action unless the thought is there first. Here are a few more symptoms you may be able to add to your list of weaknesses in order to help you in your search: procrastination, pride, shyness, fearfulness, envy, jealousy, laziness, gluttony, over-achieving, workaholism, irresponsibility, perfectionism, being super responsible, a clean freak, not letting your children grow up, sexual dysfunction (whatever that may be), a know it all, selfishness, and self-centeredness.

This is just a short list in order to help you get a start. This list will be about you, not someone else, because they are on their own spiritual path. You may look at someone else though, if it helps to point out areas you may have overlooked in yourself. For example: This person does such-and-such a thing and causes me to react in this manner toward them or myself.

The main purpose of doing these lists for morals, resentments, fears, and weaknesses, is to find patterns. They're behaviors or attitudes which have been repeated over and over again with little or no success. These behaviors and attitudes may or may not be harmful. Do not be too discouraged when looking at these lists, because they also hold the seeds to your greatest assets. Remember when we talked a little bit ago about nothing being right or wrong. It's your perspective of the rightness or wrongness of them which needs to be turned around. I don't care what weakness you may have, one of two things can be done about them. The first is to have them changed into assets; the second is to have them totally removed.

In recognizing these personality traits, we begin to own them. We will be picking them up, so as to let go of them. As was previously pointed out, you can't let go of something you haven't yet picked up and embraced. You are trying to define the Big Picture through your own lens of spiritual optics, because all answers do come from within. If you want to find God and this power to change, it has to come from within.

Once we see these patterns, we can begin to look at the underlying attitudes that set these patterns into motion. There's no action without thinking about it first. Before one can build a house, one has to first envision it. It's a law of nature; for every action there is an equal and opposite reaction. Every time our pride is threatened, fear will be there in spades. The same applies for resentment as well; there's retaliation waiting in the wing. Dr. Jung (the father of modern psychology) made the assertion that all behavior is "goal oriented." In other words, I only do something when there's something in it for me. Why do I help my wife out with her work when she's not feeling well?

First off, it's the right thing to do, and secondly, it makes me feel good to be able to help. Whatever the reason, there's something in it for me. There is some type of emotional payoff in it. We all do it; it's in our nature. Do you think much would be accomplished in this world today without the thought of getting a reward of some type? All accomplishments and defeats can be traced back to this single behavior: *There has to be something in it for me or else I'm not interested.*

Why have I written this book? There's something in it for me. That something is that my life's experiences will have had purpose; they will not have been for naught. I'll have been able to share some of the golden nuggets I've been given which have worked so well in changing my life one-hundred eighty degrees from where it was. The struggle with the great I AM is a lot easier to go through if I know that maybe in some way it will be a comfort or help to someone else who is going through the same thing. My behavior is goal oriented.

God knows we're goal oriented. He made us that way for a reason; nothing is by chance. Life uses this natural behavior in us when we're seeking to know and understand Life. Why would we want to seek the spiritual? We seek the spiritual because there's something in it for us. What's the reward? I believe the reward is freedom to experience just who we are, as well as freedom from want, freedom from the shadow side of ourselves, and finally freedom to just be at one with the All.

Strengths:

We're getting toward the end of the lists, but there's still two to go. The next item is a list of your strengths. Sometimes this can be a hard list to make because we lack humility. Remember, humility is seeing ourselves for who we really are. There's not a person born yet who doesn't have some good characteristics. We may come up short in many areas of our lives, but there has to be some assets we can capitalize on and use to good purpose. Maybe we're a good listener; put it on the list. How about stopping by the roadside to help someone who's in trouble? What if one of your strengths is being a good mediator between two opposing parties, whether in the family circle or at a conference table with labor unions?

Other possible strengths you might have is being a good parent and taking the time to do things with your children, or listening to them when they have a problem. How about being a good manager of employees or knowing how to provide a good living for yourself and your family? Or dropping change in the Salvation Army bucket, or maybe helping a senior citizen across the road? Or maybe fighting for a just cause? The list can go on and on.

Why is such a list of strengths so important? They're important because you're seeking to get a balanced view of your life. You need to get away from seeing yourself so negatively. It's no different than when it's time to clean out the garage because you can't use it for its intended purpose. You need to go through the stuff you've accumulated over time and see what can be of use.

If there's an old pile of lumber that's been laying there for years and you haven't used it, then get rid of it. That makes room for something that may be of more use down the road. Maybe you find an old garden hose with a hole in it. If it can't be used and you're not going to fix it, then get rid of it. But then again, maybe you find a set of golf clubs that hasn't been used in years because you're too busy with life. Pull them out, clean them up, and go for a round or two at the local golf course. So it is with things in your personal life, you need to make an assessment of them and ask yourself if they are turning out the way you'd like them to. Are the tools for your journey working, do they need to be sharpened, maybe polished a bit, or maybe just thrown out and replaced with new and more efficient ones?

What we need to do is take stock of the things that are in our lives. We need to see what's of use and what's not. A lot of times, when taking stock of our personal lives and seeing what our debits are, the assets will be more easily seen and used. Just as in cleaning out the garage, the more junk we can identify and either fix, use, or dispose of, the more we'll find what's valuable to us and capitalize on them.

Just pick up the pieces and go on is a common saying we've all heard a time or two in our lives. We usually hear it from a friend or a loved one after some personal crisis and we're having a hard time dealing with the loss. Let's think for a moment about this saying. First off, I would eliminate the word "just." Using that word sends the connotation that it's a relatively easy thing to do. If it's a personal dilemma or issue you're dealing with, it's never easy! Picking up the pieces is a good thing to do, but then what? What do you do with the pieces? I believe we should look at the pieces, analyze them, find out what went wrong, and if it's repairable, find a way to do that. If it's not repairable, dispose of it and get on with life. Who wants to carry around a bunch of broken pieces of life?

This is what this saying's really telling us: It's no big deal, pick up this pile of life pieces and carry it with you for the rest of your life. Common sense says if it's pieces of something, there's going to be a lot of sharp edges to it, and sharp edges cause pain. So what this is really telling us to do is to pick up these pieces with sharp edges (emotional pain pricks) and go on with life. I say, "Carefully pick up the pieces, look at them, repair them if possible, and if not repairable, then throw them away." If nothing is repairable, all is not lost. They've been here for a purpose, which is to experience them for just what they are. It's all part of your journey of enlightenment, and that's always good.

Hopes & Dreams:

The last list to make is your personal hopes and dreams. Why hopes and dreams? In the previous lists, you should have learned a lot about yourself and something outside of yourself (when in reality it's inside of you) that can help make you whole again. You should have seen many patterns come to the surface. You should be able to see the *why* of what you do and how you act or react to situations. I want to take a minute here and discuss the word "react."

Re-action is the process of acting the same way over and over again. If this is in a positive light then it's a good thing, and you'll want to seek even better. Alternatively, when a reaction is not positive, then you're banging your head against the wall, thinking that next time it's going to be different and it won't hurt as bad. This is insanity my friends. Thinking things will be different, but going about doing them

A Journey of Remembering

the same old way is a form of insanity. A sane mind would identify the results as not so good and change things to achieve the original desired results, meaning growth and moving on. So after getting a clearer picture here, we will need to act according to the moment. Stop *re-acting*.

Back to why hope and dreams? It appears I didn't answer the question in the last paragraph, so I'll try to here. Hope is the springboard of all creation. If we don't have hope, we lack dreams and when we lack dreams, we've lost sight of our soul's direction. What is there to shoot for if we can't define the target? Many of us have been taught since early on not to dream too big because it probably won't come true anyway. Hogwash, go for top-shelf! Don't settle for second-hand spirituality and don't limit God! He wants us to have the best and ultimate, whatever we personally define that to be. Dare to dream your wildest and grandest dreams and then go for it, but take God with you. Remember, He's the one who's making all this possible. Going back over these lists, we can see very clearly where we stand today. We can then begin to hope that it doesn't have to stay the same way; there may be a different and better way to do things. We begin to hope even in what may seem to be a hopeless situation. God bless you in your endeavors.

A Journey of Remembering

CHAPTER 8: TURNING DEBITS INTO ASSETS

Even the prettiest roses have thorns.

Don't be discouraged when digging up all you have on these lists. There's a Power that cannot only fix each and every one of these weaknesses of character, but most important, turn them into assets. There's not one thing on the first four lists that doesn't have a good opposite side to it. What do I mean by that? I will give you a personal example to illustrate.

As I pointed out earlier, one of my more glaring weaknesses of character was being overly prideful. I tended to take way too much credit for the good things in my life; I would flaunt them if I could. If you didn't notice what my good points were, then I'd surely point them out to you. This is not good pride; this is being haughty. It's going the extra mile to prove to everyone around me I was better than him or her, or so I thought. The opposite side of this type of pride is accepting something good in my life as being there not so much by my own making but of a Designer larger than me. The following story is a personal example of this.

With the summer of 1990 bringing me my first year of sobriety, I reached a crossroads in my life. I decided to take a spiritual sojourn of sorts with some friends in order to get away for a little while. Our trip was cut short due to a death in the family of one of my friends, so we came back early. Anyway, we decided to take another trip back out west a month or so later. After seeing all the sights, we began the trip home.

As my girlfriend (Vickie) and I were traveling down the

interstate, talking and discussing our personal lives in general, the thought came to me straight out of the blue I should go to school to be a taxidermist. I told Vickie this and she thought it would be a good thing for me. As we drove on I couldn't help but wonder where in the hell that thought came from. It had never before entered my mind. Sure, I was into nature and hunting for some time, but surely that couldn't be the reason. Yes, I admired seeing stuffed animals in museums and sports shops, but never once did I have the thought I'd like to go to school to learn how to do it someday. I was excited nonetheless. I felt I had focus in my life and things didn't have to stay the same old way, but still the old self kicked in.

My mind raced about trying to find every excuse it could to *not* go to school. I had no idea where there would be a school for taxidermy, and of course my mind said right away it would be too far away. Upon arriving home, I checked into it and there was a tech school a little over one hundred miles away. I could drive back and forth each day, even though it would be tough. Okay, so that issue was out of the way. The next thought to come was I can't afford to go to college, no matter how close to home. But after doing a little checking and filling out some paper work, I was eligible for a grant and some loans from the government.

The last big hurtle to come was how was I going to manage going to school and running my business at the same time. I had some dear friends who stepped in and said they would help do whatever I needed done. So here I was, all excuses swept away and I was enrolling in school to learn taxidermy. I didn't know if I could do it, but it was time to find out.

Part of the curriculum was learning to mount birds (waterfowl, birds of prey, all sorts). I needed to take a deceased animal and make it look lifelike again. In order to do this I needed to preserve the hide, mount it, and position it to look like it was in its natural state. About this same time a state taxidermy show and competition was fast approaching in Iowa, so I began practicing bird mounting. I also needed to get one ready in time for the show. The show's a competition which is judged by some of the top taxidermists in the world as to the quality of the competitor's mounting skills. There were three divisions which I could enter: novice, professional, and master. Awards would be given for first, second, and third place in each division.

After I decided on which bird I was going to display (or I should say birds because I had a pair of Harlequin ducks I was working on), I asked my instructor if he thought my ducks were good enough to enter into a higher division than novice (which everyone else in the class was entering). He said it was up to me, but he thought I could compete in the Professional division. So I thought to myself, "Why not?" I worked very hard as I primped and preened the birds so they'd look just right for the judges.

A couple of weeks passed by and off we went to the Iowa show. We needed to set up our display mounts and then leave the premises while the judges wrote their critiques of our mounting skills. We wouldn't know the results until the next day, at which time we'd be invited back in. The next morning arrived with me eagerly anticipating the day. I was so excited to go see how well I'd done on my entry. As Vickie and I walked past other mounts with various colored ribbons hanging on them, my anticipation began to build. I could see blue (1st), red (2nd), and yellow (3rd) ribbons on the different mounts in different divisions. Since I chose to enter the Professional division, my expectations weren't too high; I was hoping for at least a yellow ribbon on the mount.

As we turned the corner to see my mount, I was dumbfounded. I looked at my display and then at Vickie in disbelief. She gave me a look of being so proud of me, no matter what it was. It was then the tears seeped from my eyes, because there lay a huge blue ribbon with *1st. Place* embossed on it. I couldn't believe it!

Even after going over the critique sheet with the judge, I still couldn't believe it. I was so proud God had blessed me with a natural talent, a talent I didn't even know I possessed. For me, this was good pride since I was able to recognize that something had happened that I didn't have a whole lot to do with. I did the best I could with the Higher Power's help, and I was rewarded beyond my own imagination. The whole experience was very spiritual in nature. It was like a tap on the shoulder from God saying: "You know Nate, you're doing all right!"

What's so spiritual about winning a blue ribbon? Up until this time, I didn't believe I possessed the talent to do this quality of work, and as a matter of fact, I didn't believe I had much going for me at all in life. I was in my first year of sobriety and I was going through a divorce, working, and going to school all at the same time. It was an extremely tough period for me. I felt like a failure as a husband and father, I was driving 225 miles a day to go to school and trying to run a business at the same time, not to mention trying to get back into the real world after sobering up. I was also addressing many issues that were on my own lists. "God help me!" came to mind most often during this very long year.

The whole spiritual part of it was the Higher Power was giving me some kind of inner strength so I could work through it all and come out a better man on the other side. He put so many things into motion so I could do this work of spiritual growth. He made it financially possible to go to school, he put people into my life to help me get through the divorce, and he put someone very special in my life to let me know that no matter what, she was proud of me for just trying to better my life. There's spirituality in all areas of our lives if we just take the time to see it, or feel it for that matter.

No matter what roadblock the old-self put up, the Higher Power was there to make a road around it. This is what happens when one begins to do the work of personal growth that is in essence, spiritual growth. The great self or I AM doesn't want growth to happen; it's afraid of losing its identity. As you can see by this short story of mine, God works in many different ways; sometimes in very subtle ways.

During those first couple of years of early sobriety, many of the things on my own lists began to rear their ugly heads and fear topped the list. I was afraid I couldn't do the class work because of burning too many brain cells from all the years of drinking and drugging. I was also very afraid of being out in the real world. How was I going to cope with life on life's terms? I sported a good track record up to this point of not being able to deal with life successfully; I always sought to escape it. Another fear of mine was being alone; I wasn't much of a loner. I virtually had another human being around me in most everything I did. This was going to be a new adventure while attending school in a different state where I knew no one. And so the adventure began with me and God, on our own.

This is an important part of spiritual growth, alone with God. There'll be times in your life when it's just that way and you're alone with God. Let me tell you this can be one of the most frightening places to be at first. For me, this was uncharted territory. I always relied on other humans or some mood-altering drug to get me through life's situations. These were higher powers of a sort. They had to be done away with because they couldn't fix what was really wrong with me in the long run.

A Journey of Remembering

CHAPTER 9: SHARING OUR LIFE'S STORY

When you're up to your ass in alligators, don't forget your objective which is to drain the swamp!

So now what do we do after we've made these lists of our lives? Very simply, we need to share them with one other human being and God. This may sound like a drastic step and I agree it is, but if you want the spiritual rewards, sometimes it requires drastic measures. This part of your spiritual growth will probably require every bit of personal fortitude you have, and also a lot of help from the Higher Power. This can be a very fearful process. This is where you begin to bring your will in line with that of Life. Remember how we discussed the ability of God to turn these weaknesses into assets a while back? Well, this is where you allow Him to take your own self-will and turn it into something that can be put to good use.

Why is this part of the process so fearful? For myself, I took great pride in the fact that not one single person knew my whole life's story. You could take the few close friends or family members around me at the time, ask them all about me, and you could hear about seventy-five percent of the real me. The other twenty-five percent I kept hidden. Why did I keep it hidden? I was fearful of what others would think of me if they knew the real me; I would be rejected on the spot. Very little respect was shown me in the first place and I wasn't going to make it any worse with my own words. At the time, I shared Abraham Lincoln's philosophy: *"Better to remain silent and be thought a fool than to speak out and remove all doubt."*

A Journey of Remembering

Another reason I kept things hidden is feeling they just wouldn't understand. Don't get me wrong, there were people in my life that tried to break down the walls I built and help me; I just couldn't drop the barriers. I was definitely afraid of rejection. I reasoned these other people didn't live the life I had, so how could they understand? When finding someone else to share your lists with, you need to take some time to find someone you can trust, who will be non-judgmental and loving. They'll need a good relationship with the Higher Power in order to be helpful as you pursue this task.

This may look like a confession of sorts, and yes you're partly right. But confession is only a *symptom* of what you're doing. One part of what you're doing here is *ex-pressing* what's inside of you. You're pushing it out; you're claiming it as your own. Once you claim something from the dark side of your personality, it's brought into the light where you allow it to go. Another thing you're doing is trying to get to your right size. It's a lesson in humility (not humiliation). In discussing these lists you've so carefully thought out and put down on paper, you'll be able to see many reasons *why* you were doing the things you did and probably continue to do.

You'll be able to get down to the root causes of those weaknesses in your character. This is why you need to pick someone who understands what you're trying to accomplish. Another reason you'll need to discuss these lists with another human being is to show the Higher Power your pride is no longer in the way. You'll need some measure of humility to complete this process. So before you start this phase of the journey, it's advisable to say a prayer to the Higher Power and invite Him in to be with you in this undertaking. You'll need His help to see yourself for who you really are (the good and the bad), and to guide the person you choose to share these lists with.

I know we've talked about this before, but I feel it's very important we go over it again, because all of us have secrets known only to ourselves. These secrets may be of some behavior you participated in which was against what you believed in at the time, or maybe the secret is of some thought you had which seemed to go against your own moral code. It doesn't matter what the secret is though, it's what the secret *does to you* that matters. Secrets will alienate you from those around you. You may see these particular secrets as something bad, something you have to keep to yourself so no one ever finds out, secrets that go to the grave with you.

These secrets make you live in constant fear until they're brought out into the light. You may forever pretend there's nothing wrong and yet deep down inside, you know there is (or at least that's what you perceive). These secrets may not even be about you; they could be about a loved one, a loved one you've taken upon yourself to protect. Thus you live in fear for them and yourself, but do these secrets actually cause that much harm? I personally believe those secrets no one else is to know will take you to the grave (instead of you taking them) earlier than planned. Again in short, secrets kill!

I am often amazed at what lengths humans will go to so no one will ever find out. My personal philosophy at the time was to admit nothing and deny everything. And that's the way I lived my life for thirty some years. What would people think of me if they ever found out my secrets? I lived in terror because of this sort of thinking. Some of my secrets would do great damage to others if found out, or so I thought. I had to keep them from prying eyes. Most of all, my secrets would do great harm to myself. How's that? My pride would take a terrible blow if these things were found out. How would I ever be able to walk around with my head up, even though I couldn't do that at the time anyway?

Another reason for the process of self-appraisal is being able to get a clear view of your self through another human's eyes. While telling them the story of your life, they're able to see from an outsider's point of view what may *really* be wrong. Because of many years of rationalization or justification for your unproductive behaviors, you probably can't see things as clearly as you should, because fear and pride will be there big time trying to halt the process.

The person we're sharing this with may be able to see some things we didn't even know are there. I'll give you a personal example of this. Looking at my resentment list, I started with my father, as he headed the list. Why would I have resentment against him? I hated him because he was a stiff disciplinarian. No, make that abusive. In today's society he would be sitting in jail for child abuse. He treated me badly, even brutally.

Early, early childhood seemed okay as far as I could remember, but somewhere along the way things changed between my father and me. On one occasion he caught me licking the frosting off a piece of cake I had on my plate (you never did that in our family, you ate the cake and the frosting as one piece). Anyway, my punishment for this "crime" was to drink a four-quart pan of water straight down with no arguments about it. Well, I'll tell you what, that volume of water in a six-year-old body is damn near impossible to do and to be honest, I don't remember if I drank it all. All I remember thinking at the time is someday I will get that son-of-a-bitch back.

On another occasion, he caught me playing with a book of matches. He offered no explanation as to what playing with matches could do or the harm it could cause. He just snatched the book of matches away from me and lit one and demanded I take it. I hesitantly took the lit match and he told not to let go of it until it burned out, even if it went all the way down to my fingers! And so it went with the other sixteen matches in the book (yes, I counted them). My pointing finger and thumb were black and hard on the ends from being burnt so badly. But you know what? I wouldn't give him the satisfaction of seeing me cry. I'd be damned if I was going to let him get to me.

On another occasion, after being told not to spit on the sidewalk, I did it again without even thinking about it and he happened to be there at the time. Again, it was time to suffer the punishment of whatever he felt like doing at the time. I didn't have to wait long for the sentence. He proceeded to clear his throat and spit that shit right in my face; there can't be anything more humiliating or dehumanizing than that!

Another time I was playing in the sand box out back of the house when my father called for me to come in and eat supper. Well, being a normal kid who wanted to finish what I was doing, I didn't jump right up and run for the dinner table. After hearing the back door of the house explode open as he came through it and seeing fire radiate out of his narrowing grey eyes, I knew I was screwed and it was too late to run. As a sidenote, I wouldn't have run anyway because I knew I'd get it twice as bad; you just didn't run away from the old man.

A Journey of Remembering

All of us kids (my brothers and sisters) knew when was he out to teach one of us a lesson. He was like a lion which has already decided on its prey; you just knew something bad was going to happen. He adamantly walked over to where I was innocently playing and proceeded to pick up a steel toy shovel that was lying there and began beating my back with it. After five or six blows that knocked the wind out of me and left a deep burning sensation, he grabbed my left ear, picked me up by it, and physically carried me to the house while my feet dangled in midair. Anyway, this is just a small sampling of things that happened in my years of growing up. I won't go into any deeper detail for you to get the message of why I harbored a nasty resentment against him.

As I was discussing these situations with the person I chose to hear my story, he sat back and listened very patiently and with great understanding and love; he was neither condemning, nor judgmental. After I was done describing these hurts and injustices done to me over the seventeen years I lived at home, he asked me about my paternal grandfather. What kind of a man was he? I told him by the time I was old enough to remember my grandfather he quit drinking and became a gentle old man, but from other family members I was able to pry out (family secrets, you know?) the fact he was not always the gentle old man whom I'd grown to love. As a matter of fact, he was the complete opposite. He had some real brutal sexual problems and I also found out he'd been very abusive with my father and his siblings.

The spiritual advisor who was listening to me told me everything my father did to me, he learned from my grandfather. Then he asked me where I thought my grandfather learned them from, and so on backwards in time. I caught on as to what he was trying to get me to see. How could I put so much blame on someone who was doing just what he'd seen and thus been taught, with the same consideration applied to my grandfather, and my great-grandfather, and so on back in time? This is how the "sins of the father" are visited upon his children while they perpetuate them onto the generations that follow. It never ends until one generation says, "Enough!"

After realizing how much blame and hatred my father was receiving from me for the injustices done, it became real hard for me to put the blame on anyone specific. Who do you blame? Do you blame him, his father, or his father's father, or his father's grandfather? Where does it end? How many times did I perpetuate the sins of my father onto my own children? It didn't matter anymore who started it; I just knew it had to be stopped!

When all the blaming is done and it's time to develop a different and better way of living, change will occur. I decided right then and there I was no longer going to live in my father's shadow. I finally became a person with a little hair on my ass, so-to-speak. Now was the time to start building the new Nathan and in that process somewhere, I learned to forgive. I honestly don't know when it happened, but I do know how it happened. I quit blaming. Through the process of making and talking about these lists, I found out I no longer had reason to blame my parents, religion, society, or whatever; it just didn't matter anymore. Blaming only kept me a victim and I've already discussed what victims are and how they act.

After we discussed my relationship with my father and my resentments, he asked me where my mother was when all this abuse was going on. He noticed my mother wasn't on my resentment list. I nervously laughed and said: "What are you talking about?" He asked again where my mother was all this time. I came back a little more defensive this time. Not wanting to answer him directly I said, "What does she have to do with this anyway?" He knew something, or could see something I couldn't, and I was going to find out what it was in short order.

I'll tell you what, my advisor flew out of the easy chair he was calmly sitting in and bolted across the room. He came to within inches of my nose and demanded a straight answer, "Cut-out the fucking bullshit! Where was your mom in all this?!" All of a sudden, years of well-hidden emotions came frothing forth like a dam of water bursting its containment walls. I was emotionally laid bare! I could no longer hide the "secret" of my mother's own abusive ways; it was totally out in the open now. Not only did I hold her responsible for her own abusive ways, I also held her responsible for all the abuse that I suffered from my father, while she did absolutely nothing to stop it.

Here I was; thirty years old and trying to protect the perfect

A Journey of Remembering

ideal I made up of my mother. I did love her (or so I thought), for what could she do? She was treated the same as us children. I didn't even know these emotions were there. They were buried so deep I wasn't even aware of them, but very soon afterward I was blessed with a truly healing tranquility. No longer were the secrets going to hold me for ransom.

Within minutes of these secret revelations, I was immersed in a feeling of calmness; the unbearable pain of almost two decades of abuse just vanished almost instantly. In just a few short minutes (maybe three minutes total), I went from total denial of things that happened to me by my own mother and father to a perfect healing, which is still present almost twenty years later. As the great emotional dam burst forth, a healing tranquility swept through me as if waves of water were cleansing me, washing out the hatred and damnation I felt toward my parents. Sad to say, it took almost twenty-five years to come to this part of the healing process. I carried this baggage with me for so long, and only God knows how much this sub-conscience garbage made me react to different things in my life.

This garbage I carried with me for so long cut me off from the spirit of God. How did that happen? It happened when I went into early survival mode. Survival mode is when a person is willing to do almost anything (which may even include going against their own moral code of conduct) to survive on their *own* power. In order for me to get out of this mode, I had to see who I was all about; I had to see it through another person's eyes and own it. We have to be rid of these secrets if we're to truly live a life that's not one big lie. There'll be no serenity, no peace of mind, and there'll be no happiness until we do these things; it's just that simple. If I expected to reap the spiritual rewards, I had to do the personal house cleaning.

Now let's explore who's to hear your story. I need to stress very strongly here that you'll need to take great care while choosing this person. Here's a bit of advice: it wouldn't be a dumb thing to ask God for guidance in this area. Ask Him to point out someone who He thinks should hear this. A Buddhist proverb points out *"When the student is ready, the teacher will appear."* Characteristics of this teacher should be someone who can keep a confidence about the things you talk about, while at the same time be understanding and considerate of what you're trying to accomplish.

When you go to them, state the exact mission you're on. Some choices to consider might be the minister in your church, or perhaps a counselor or psychologist you're familiar with. If you do choose someone outside the clergy, make sure they have a good spiritual basis with which to help you. They'll need to keep an open mind about things you need to talk about. One other thing I should stress here is a clergy person, counselor, doctor, or psychologist, in most cases can't be subpoenaed in a court of law to reveal the things you've talked about; it has to do with patient/client confidentiality. There may be things you need to disclose which may have been against the law, but you should not let these things keep you from doing what you need to do.

One other thing I'll add to this is, whomever you chose to hear your story, they will most assuredly be honored you've chosen them to help in this endeavor. I've been much honored when people have asked me to help them through this difficult task of trying to make heads-or-tails of their life. I can't describe the feeling of being trusted with this truly life-and-death errand. I've also been filled with a great measure of gratitude toward God for directing them to me. In the end, you must be willing to go to any length to get the spiritual rewards that are yours for the taking.

What are the spiritual rewards you can have? Right around this part of the spiritual process, you'll begin to feel a nearness to your Creator. You'll feel forgiveness for harms done to others and to yourself. The Higher Power will begin to do for you what no one or nothing has been able to do before or ever will. He'll begin to heal you from the inside out. No longer will you have to hide from yourself or others. You'll begin to have a spiritual experience and I'm here to tell you this feeling is *the single greatest thing* on earth or in heaven! It being a spiritual experience while in human form, you combine the spiritual and physical planes, resulting in an entirely new life form.

Spiritual experiences come in many forms. You may have the variety that consists of feelings of total peace and serenity. No, I take that back, you may *experience* firsthand what perfect peace, serenity,

A Journey of Remembering

and oneness with the Creator is. It's extremely strong and forceful. This variety will put you on your knees in total gratitude and humbleness. You'll never be the same after this, thank God!

Another variety may be the educational type. By educational type I mean over time you'll learn to see what the Higher Power has done for you in ways you couldn't have done for yourself. Neither of the two experiences is any better or worse than the other. Frequently, the spiritual experiences you'll have may be intermingled. I choose not to go into any more detail on spiritual experiences, because I don't want to mislead you with the idea they have to happen in certain ways, or else they're not a true experience. Experiences such as these are customized to each individual's needs and prior experiences.

If you would like to do further research on the subject of spiritual experiences, I suggest you read William James' book, *The Varieties of Religious Experiences*. He goes into great detail as to the many kinds of spiritual experiences one can have. One thing will be true of all true spiritual experiences though, they'll make you see things totally different than the way you've been used to. Everything will have changed, yet nothing will have changed. You'll begin to see through a new set of spiritual eyes. The things in the material plane will not matter all that much, because the things in the material plane will have found their proper place; they'll all be a means to an end instead of ends to a means.

Spiritual experiences do have varying degrees of strength though, but one thing is for sure, they'll forever change you, sometimes subtly, other times drastically. To be labeled a true spiritual experience, it has to bring about positive change though, for God's ways are perfect. He would never change us for the worse.

A Journey of Remembering

CHAPTER 10: BEING READY FOR THE HIGHER POWER

*Everyone wants to go to heaven,
but no one wants to die!*

There's still more spiritual work for you to do now. Don't delay or forget to do this next part of the process, as this part can be easily forgotten after all you've just been through. This is where you become entirely ready to ask God to have *all* of you, including those parts you've kept hidden or didn't know about, and also all the good things you've discovered while sharing your story.

After reviewing my life's story and all it entailed, I was surely ready to have God fix it all. After a lifetime of trying to fix myself, the results were not too thrilling to see. I don't see how any person, after taking a good hard look at their life and seeing where self-reliance has taken them, can't help but be ready for change. Personally, I was sick and tired of hurting those about me and seeing the damage I caused in their lives and my own. A life built around self-will invariably causes great damage to the surrounding area. Deep down inside, this is what we all run from. We run from the guilt and shame for things done, things that if we had the chance to do over we would surely do differently.

This phase of your spiritual work doesn't require much effort. Upon arriving home after your long talk with your spiritual advisor, find a place of quiet. You need to sit down and carefully review everything that was discussed and looked at. How do you feel about it? Was it done do the best of your ability? Did you knowingly leave anything out? Did you become aware of the patterns and trends in your character? Did you find out the root causes of your behaviors? If after personally reviewing the lists and all you have gained from them, you notice something that was missed, pick up the phone or go back to see the person you talked to, and get it out into the open.

You must be vigilant in this part of the process. You're now building a new dwelling of sorts. Is the foundation on solid ground, cemented with your best honesty and humility? It wouldn't be too wise to use inferior material in this part of the building process because everything to come will be based on how well the foundation has been laid. If you let fear stop you from your appointed growth, you need to redouble your efforts and ask God to help you to be less fearful.

So now after reviewing all, you are content with what you've just accomplished and you've been able to come to terms with the real you, then waste no more time. Put your lists and notes away and offer a prayer to the Higher Power. Make up your very own, for you're probably meeting God for the first time in your earthly live; at least the first time since you have gained new conceptions of Him and yourself.

This is the one-on-one relationship that Jesus lived and died for. One of the main reasons of His life was to do away with all the pomp and circumstance of religions. He opened a shortcut to God. We don't need all the ceremonial pageantry we see in churches these days. This is a simple process of spiritual truth and growth. By this time of your process you will have come to a new and much better understanding of your Creator.

In case you're having a hard time coming up with a prayer, try and fashion one around the following: "Dear God, I've done my very best in finding the real me. I've discussed it with another human being, and I'm now ready for You to have *all* of me. Please remove from me all you may find objectionable to the doing of our will and our purpose here on the earthly plane. Please grant me the strength to bring my will in line with Yours, Peace." Short, sweet, and to the point. Keep it as simple as you see fit. God doesn't require too hard of terms to meet Him. It's kind of a quirky thing. In order to claim God's grace in your life, you must first do the groundwork to make sure it falls on fertile soil.

After the prayer, find time to get some rest because your physical body will have gone through quite a bit of stress. You'll sleep like you've never slept before, because now you're at perfect ease with the Creator and great things are apt to happen very shortly! Don't expect to be rendered white as snow when you turn your life and your self-will over to the care and love of the Higher Power. It would be like a teacher giving you all the answers to the questions on the tests and then passing you on to the next level. That's not a fair or loving thing to do.

What you'll gain though is the power to live life on life's terms, whatever that might be for you personally. Remember, we're all here to grow spiritually and to experience life as we create it. Life will give us the tools and the knowledge we'll need as we need it. This is where self-will is brought into line with the will of the God. You'll be able to exert all the self-will you need to, as long as it's in line with what your soul needs. If you're exerting your self-will and not accomplishing anything, then it's time to take a break and look at the situation. Does it go along with the will of the Higher Power? If not, then you need to pray for direction and guidance so as to be able to bring it into conformity with His.

Another reason you'll not be rendered snow white is the Higher Power and you may still have use for some of your so-called character weaknesses in the work He's doing through you. These weaknesses will be transformed when they need to be, not a second sooner. What we should be content with is steady improvement of them, because while we seek spiritual perfection, we'll patiently settle for spiritual progress no matter how slow it seems to us.

I can't go much further in discussing spirituality without letting you know what happened to me after I completed my own inventory and offered myself to the Higher Power as I understood Him at the time. The discussion of my list with my spiritual advisor took from about 7:30 p.m. on a Thursday evening until around 6:00 the following Friday morning. Needless to say, I was exhausted. I did my quiet time while reflecting on things we discussed and then I said my prayer. I soon fell fast asleep. I woke up sometime in the early afternoon. I felt rested, yet I felt I had been shoved through a knot-hole backwards. I thought I better tend to my business and get some work done. It took me a couple of hours to really "come to" in a sense, and then it began! Just writing those previous three words makes the hair stand up on my arms.

It was like nothing I had ever experienced before. I felt as if I were out on the ocean and with each passing wave of water, I was being pushed further and further ashore until I was able to stand on dry ground. Each wave brought new feelings and awareness. I cried most of the next three days. They were tears of total gratitude, gratitude for *everything* that happened to me and *everything* I had been through. It was so overwhelming, but in a good sense! I experienced a feeling of forgiveness for everything I did wrong because I forgave those who mistreated me.

What a humbling experience! God loved me and He cared for me. I had often been told that by other people but I never *felt* it. As the saying goes, *no sense, no feel.* He just needed to have me ask for His help. I needed to remove the great I AM and surrender to the powers that be. The humbling part of it all was the Higher Power wanted me just as I was; not the made up Nathan, but the real me. I always thought God wanted perfect people.

During those three days, I experienced a life review and a short glimsp of the future. No matter what I thought of from things in the past, there was a perfect answer for why it all happened. I *experienced and knew* why the things happened to me in the order they did. It all made perfect sense to me. There was a much Greater Plan involved here which I had no imagination of whatsoever. I also *knew* I was done sacrificing because I no longer needed to do things the hard way.

There was a way out of this dysfunctional life I was trying to orchestrate. I didn't have to keep losing things anymore. I was shown a perfect order of sorts; ninety-nine percent of the crap I used to get so upset about in life didn't matter anymore because there was a Divine Purpose now and I was part of it, just as we all are. When God comes to you, you will *know*! You will *experience* Him in all His glory. As my spiritual advisor always pointed out, *"If you think you know, you don't know, but when you know, you know!"*

With this spiritual experience lasting longer than I thought it should (preconceived idea), I began to think I was losing my mind and I guess in a sense, I was. My mind and soul were now being used by the Creator in His purpose for both of us. Anyway, I called my advisor because I couldn't believe what was happening to me, nor did I know what was happening to me. To be quite honest, it kind of scared the shit out of me. I'd done some really good drugs in my day and nothing even came close to this! This experience wasn't stopping or subsiding, nor could I make it stop even if I wanted to. When God has a hold of you, He doesn't let go easily. He really knows how to hug; it was as if a parent were hugging their child after a very long absence.

Anyway, I called my advisor and tried to describe to him what was going on in me. I told him I felt a little foolish because I couldn't quit crying these tears of joy. I asked him what the hell was happening to me. He just laughed and said I wasn't going crazy, I was just having a spiritual experience. "Enjoy it as long as it lasts," he replied. "Wow! What a relief, I thought I was going crazy," was my reply. And like a good teacher that my advisor was, he shared my tears of joys with me, because now his own trials and tribulations made more sense to him. Everything he experienced was for good purpose also. This is the way spirituality works; we all get to share in it. Even my wife knew something wonderful happened because she wept tears of joy too. Now I was sharing and experiencing something she experienced herself long before we met. She always told me, "God may shut a door, but He always leaves a window open. You just have to look to find it sometimes."

It was also at this time I felt what I had left at that exact moment was what God and I were going to use to build a new life which has sense and purpose. This wasn't going to be a new life which would be squandered. It was going to be of good use from then on. Nothing would be the same, and yet to all outward appearances, nothing changed. I've been very blessed to see this experience happen to other people in my life and I can tell when things have changed for them. They seem to have a "glow" about them; they have been transformed in a sense. No longer are they set out to do their own will, but the will of life and love.

Are these types of experiences only for a chosen few? I think not. They're available to anyone who chooses to go down the path of spiritual enlightenment. It's for the masses but only a few will choose to take it. Why is this? Choosing this path requires much effort and work on your part. It requires a burning desire for something better than what you presently have. It requires a desire to *know and experience* the Creator; it's that simple. I do see it happening more and more though. Just take a few minutes in your local bookstore and you'll see the new age of spirituality coming on. It is the age of the new millennium.

    I will leave this chapter with the following thought from Dr. Bob (co-founder of Alcoholics Anonymous): "I sought my God - My God eluded me. I sought my Soul - My Soul I could not see. I sought my brother - I found all three."

A Journey of Remembering

CHAPTER 11: CLEANING UP THE PAST

*"Before spiritual enlightenment, chop wood, carry water.
After spiritual enlightenment, chop wood, carry water." –
Old Zen Parable*

Now's not the time to rest on your spiritual laurels, because the spiritual life is based on ever forward spiritual advancement. A lake with no river running into it or out of it will soon become stagnant. So it is with us humans, we must forge ahead for we're now on new spiritual footing. We'll be working in concert with the Higher Power now, not against Him. If we're open to His spirit, He'll guide our actions and thoughts. He'll now give to you by His grace the means to begin construction of the new home for His indwelling spirit, and what a new home it'll be!

As the foundation of this new home has already been laid, it's now time to begin construction of the upper stories in which you'll dwell. After taking this life-changing look at your past and present, you'll to come to terms with the fact there's been some destruction in your life and the lives of those around you. A life based on self-will causes great damage to your personal environment. You'll need to sort through the debris and see if there's anything salvageable, and then repair the harm done to the best of your ability.

How do we go about this part of the process? Part of this should have already been done. You should have a list of harms done from the list you shared with another human being and God. When you listed these resentments, morals, fears, and weaknesses, you should've found out how these parts of your character adversely affected those around you. If you did a good job on these lists and in turn discussed them with someone else, you can't help but see the damage done because of your behaviors and attitudes. You'll need a willingness to set right the wrongs done by you.

What purpose is served by repairing the harms done to others? The harms done to others are the symptoms of your behaviors. So as to not repeat the same behaviors and cause still more damage, you need to set about righting these past wrongs by changing the attitudes which set them in motion in the first place. Maybe one of the harms done is to a parent with whom you've been engaged in a bitter feud with for many years. By going to them and making amends for your own wrongs toward them, the spirit of forgiveness can set in and probably will. After opening up the discussion, the years of built up walls of indifference can begin to come down.

We need to at least make an honest attempt in this area of our lives. We don't want any unusable baggage holding us back as we walk this new road to spiritual and personal freedom. We're not to concern ourselves with their wrongs or misdeeds because we can't do anything about them; these are part of their own spiritual path.

What are amends for harm done? First off, we need to define what harms were set into motion. Suppose we stole (whether money or belongings) from a family member. What harms were done to them? For one thing, their security was threatened. They may now feel vulnerable because of your selfishness. Another way they may have been affected is in their trustworthiness of others. What if because of our behaviors, they begin to doubt other family members who have no reason of being untrustworthy? As our actions of selfishness (stealing) arise, it usually brings out the worst in those around us.

What if one of your weaknesses of character happens to be anger? By the way, anger is not a weakness of character; anger is only the emotion that's attached to the weakness. How we display anger though, is another thing. That can be a very damaging character weakness. Anger brings out the defenses of those around us, because like begets like. When someone was angry with me, I would instantly go on the defensive. If you backed me into a corner, you wouldn't like the consequences that resulted because I didn't fight fair. Right off the bat I would go straight for your jugular. This is one of my own

A Journey of Remembering

weaknesses I've turned over to God to let Him deal with as He sees fit.

Anyway, I always thought it was wrong to get angry, at least that was the idea I was given by my parents, religion, and society. After doing some research in the Good Book, I read where Jesus went into the temple and began throwing the moneychangers and their booths or tables around because he felt they were defiling the house of His Father. What's going on here? Here was this supposedly perfect human being who became so angry He got violent enough to overturn tables and such. That just didn't seem to fit the ideas I was taught.

I was preached at to be Christ-like, yet I wasn't to be angry when I saw injustices happening. The religious folks didn't like it when I pointed out Jesus' behavior in the temple. "He's different," is what I was told. What I was really hearing from both the church and my parents was not to be angry at all, period. How the hell do you do that? After some more research, I found what they were telling me was not the really the way it was, because the Bible says, "*Slow* to become angry" (James 1:19). It doesn't say anything about not getting angry, it just says to be slow in getting there.

If we're not slow to anger, then we're just like a lit stick of dynamite; it's only a matter of time before we go off. But if we're slow to anger, then we have time to think the situation through, and ninety-nine percent of the time we'll see an angry response is not warranted. We need to learn to act differently and not react to an emotionally charged situation. One more thing, anger used in a right sense can be a motivating force in pursuing a strongly held conviction.

Getting back to where we were going before, you'll need to be willing to make amends for harms done. If you aren't willing at the time, that's fine; willingness will come all on its own. To amend something means to change it. Take for instance our Constitution of the United States. If the population as a whole finds something that's disagreeable in the constitution, then the citizens vote to have the constitution amended or changed to something that's more agreeable to society. The making of amends is not running around saying, "I'm sorry for this or that." Amends are about making positive changes. Amends may also include some restitution for the actual harm caused by one's behavior, whether that is money, time, or both.

A Journey of Remembering

Before we get the cart before the horse, we need to slow down a bit. First off, you can't go around admitting all these harms done to other people and not care about the consequences of this behavior. If you don't proceed cautiously, there's a strong possibility of doing even greater damage to those harmed in the first place. Take for instance this example: Let's say you embezzled some money from the business you worked for, and you felt some restitution was necessary for harm caused to the company. Should you hop on your white horse and gallop over to speak with your boss while explaining what you've done? What if the company doesn't see your repentance as fondly as you do, and then promptly fires you and seeks legal recourse? What happens to your family you're providing for in the meantime? What good is this going to do them if you become unemployable because of this behavior?

You need to look at situations like this very carefully and weigh all the possibilities and consequences of your actions as regards to how this affects others who are dependant on you. You need to talk to your spiritual advisor and family to get their input on it. If it only affects yourself, you need to bite the bullet no matter what the consequences, but when others are involved you need to proceed very carefully so as to not do any more damage than what you've already done. Only a fool would proceed in spiritual matters alone.

There's such a thing called spiritual pride. What's that you ask? Spiritual pride is *thinking* since you're so spiritually aware now, you'll know what's best for all concerned. You become so pious you lose sight of what happens to others because you're on a mission of righteousness while only thinking of yourself. Spiritually speaking, humility and love will dictate what the best course of action is regarding the making of amends and how it affects others.

Part of what we're trying to achieve here in this part of the process is the forming of better relationships with those we live and socialize with. This whole spiritual process we've been discussing begins in the home. Naturally this will be the toughest place to practice it because this is where you're most vulnerable and also this is where the most damage has been done. The process is simple, but not easy to do. It will require a real willingness on your part to want something

A Journey of Remembering

better than what you've had in the past.

These amends are a lifelong process that you'll need to continue with until your earthly phase is through. If you're not changing, then you'll become stagnant like the lake with no inlet or outlet. After progressing through this part of the journey, you'll be able to walk with your head up. No longer will you have to go out of your way to avoid the people you've harmed. Maybe you're grocery shopping and up ahead you spy someone with whom you've had a bad encounter with, or did something selfish which hurt them. It's kind of funny how all of a sudden you remember to pick something up at the other end of the store just so you don't have to run into the person. I can tell you this though, once the face-to-face amends has been made, you'll no longer have to avoid that person no matter what the circumstances are.

What about the amends you can't make because maybe the person's died or they've moved away to parts unknown? Are you willing to make amends to them if you could? If you are willing to make amends even though you can't, then consider it a closed case. Tell God about it your prayers that you would make the amends if you could; I know He'll understand. Whenever you're willing to make these amends, God will provide the means and the way to do it, just leave it in His hands.

If you need to make some financial amends to someone and that's not possible because of their death, then find a relative and give it to them, or maybe find out what they died of and make a donation to the charity searching for a cure. Use your imagination, that's what God gave it to you for. This may be one of those places where you let God turn one of those character weaknesses into a positive attribute. Were you always day dreaming of an easy way to get ahead financially? Then use your imagination for good and daydream of a way to make restitution for a harm done which can't be directly amended.

Here's a personal amends I had to make. I avoided this amends for a long time because of fearing what this person would think of me for causing harm to him. There was also fear concerning my ego deflation and I wasn't looking forward to that either. It's not a lot of fun to walk up to someone and admit that you stole from them, depriving them and their family the fruits of their hard labor.

    I neatly avoided doing this amends for a number of years through purposeful forgetting and using the rationalization that I didn't have the financial resources to do it properly. My head decided that "proper" meant I should give him back all the stolen money at one time, figuring that doing it this manner would finish it once and for all. Another reason I didn't want to make the face-to-face amends was there was possible jail time involved because of the amount and the nature of the things I stole. If I admitted to this theft and he wanted to prosecute, then I would have to suffer the consequences for my behavior. Mind you, I wanted to grow spiritually, but not with too much pain!

    Do you know what this was? This was all a malarkey I cooked up in my mind in order to not do the right thing and fix a wrong. I talked it over with my wife and obtained her input on the dilemma because this gravely affected her too. She knew the spiritual journey I was on and left it up to me to make the decision as to what to do. She expressed to me if I felt that strongly about making this right, then I better talk to God and do what I had to do. God bless her, because this was something I could no longer avoid or put off. I needed to make things right no matter what the consequences. My conscience would not let me sleep anymore because of it. Life has a way of getting your attention when it needs you to do something.

    So off I went to talk to this person. God was I scared! It seemed like my whole life was on the line, and in a way it was. I asked myself if this spiritual journey was just a sham on my part or was I really going to let go of the branch and let God take care of it however He saw fit. Needless to say, I did a whole lot of praying on my drive over to see this person. God, please help me get through this, was all that kept going through my mind at the time. I was kind of hoping he wasn't home, yet asking God to see to it he was. Facing a fear with a new power in ones' life can be quite an adventure.

    Rounding the last corner in the road, I could see him loading his truck for a weekend vacation. As I pulled into his driveway I thought to myself, "Well, I can't stop now, here goes nothing." I got out of my truck and proceeded to introduce myself because it was a few years since we'd seen each other. Thankfully he remembered me and I told him my purpose for being there. I told him face-to-face I was there to right a wrong to the best of my ability. I explained to him my purpose for doing this, as I needed to get on with my life and take care of some past deeds I was not too proud of.

I didn't make any excuses for my behavior because there was none. I apologized for what happened and then handed him a pretty good sum of money to start paying him back for his losses. What happened next, I couldn't believe! He took the money, shook my hand and expressed his thankfulness to me for coming forward and owning up to my misdeed. We talked a while longer and then we were both off on our own ways. As I slowly drove away, tears began welling up in my eyes as a sense of gratitude overwhelmed me. The Higher Power was with me and He saw me through it. I was willing to pay any consequence for my act of selfishness, but God figured I paid enough already. What a relief it was. I could now see this gentleman and not run and hide from him; I could now walk with my head held high.

I just have to throw a little riddle in here. There are three frogs sitting on a log in the water. One of them decides to jump into the water. How many frogs are still sitting on the log? You'll find the answer in the back of the book. No, just kidding. Did you come up with the answer that there are two frogs left? That was my first answer too, but it wasn't correct. Actually, there are still three frogs sitting on the log. How can that be? That one frog only made a decision; that's all it was, nothing more. A decision has to be followed by an action to be completed, as in actually jumping off the log. If there's no more than a decision, then nothing has happened. There are still three frogs sitting on the log. So when making a decision to do something, act on it, and you'll get the results of your creation. There's freedom for those who make a decision and then jump. So believe and trust in your decision; jump off the log and swim.

The Higher Power can tell if you're a willing participant in this spiritual journey you're on. Spirituality is not for the faint of heart because sometimes you may have to resort to extreme measures in order to obtain the desired rewards. At times it will require great courage to trust in something outside of yourself to see you through a

A Journey of Remembering

tough situation. Be ready to expect the unexpected because when the Higher Power is working in your life, miraculous things become quite common. All you have to do is to be willing to practice some spiritual principles to the best of your ability; no matter how half-assed your progress may *seem* to be. God knows what's in your heart; He will provide.

This reminds me of one of stories we read about in the Bible. It was the story of Abraham and Isaac. The story goes that God wanted Abraham to sacrifice his only son Isaac on an altar he was to build on a way-off mountain. Abraham proceeded to gather firewood for the burnt offering of his son and when all the wood had been gathered, they were to set off on a three-day journey to the mountains. Now can you imagine what was going through Abraham's mind during this three-day journey? Not only did he have to travel for three days in mountainous terrain and carry everything for an altar, he was also thinking about the sacrifice of his only son because God wanted a demonstration of his faith.

What a load on Abraham's mind. I'm sure he didn't think right off the bat this was such a great way to show God how much he believed in Him. I'm sure he questioned the wisdom of it as I'm sure he loved his only son very much. I can't imagine what other mental torture he went through on the trek to the mountain. Yet on arrival, he set up the altar, bound his son, and laid him on the altar.

The next thing he did was pick up the knife he'd brought with him. As he was in the act of doing that (picking up the knife), God sent an angel to stop Abraham from killing his son. After unbinding his son, he noticed a ram caught in the bushes. This ram was to be used as a sacrifice instead of his son. God was so pleased with Abraham he blessed him beyond his imagination. For a more detailed account of this story, you can read it in Genesis 22:1-19. I just hit on some of the high notes of the story to emphasize a few points I've gathered from the reading.

What do I see from this story? For me, I see a whole lot of what is *not* written about. And what would that be? What was not written about were some of the personal emotional issues Abraham had to be dealing with. With Abraham being a human being, I can't

A Journey of Remembering

help but think he was not any too enthused about taking a long trip to go and kill his only son. I can't help think he might have questioned God's wisdom in this affair a time or two, but yet he plodded on knowing in the end what needed to happen.

The moral of this story is about Abraham's faith. The Good Book says, "Faith without deeds is dead" (James 2:26). In his own mind (as he gathered the wood, got provisions for the journey, made the journey, set up the altar, and finally bound his son and laid him on the altar), Abraham could see this was all footwork that had to be done. But the real demonstration of his faith was not to come until the exact moment of picking up the sharp knife and killing his son. All the things I've just mentioned up until the time of grabbing the knife were *talking* the faith, but when he grabbed the knife he began to *live* his faith. What's the difference? Anybody could have done the talking the faith parts of the journey. The acts of picking the wood, the journey, and the binding, were just that, acts as in acting; anyone could do them. They would look good to anyone who was watching; it's a show of sorts.

But what of the act of picking up that knife though? That was the living of his faith, the deeds of his faith. He reached the point where it was either do it or don't. That was the *real* demonstration of his faith in the Higher Power. At anytime before this, he could've called it off; there was always an out. He could have rationalized some way out of this sacrifice in his own mind, but he didn't. Maybe he could've put it off till a more convenient time had approached, but he didn't. This man truly deserved the blessings he received for his demonstration of faith while on his spiritual journey. Many of the experiences we have in life consist mainly of inconveniences to our journey, kind of like getting a flat tire while on vacation. Yes, some effort and time are consumed, but it's not that big a deal. Gladly there are very few actual situations where sacrifices are asked for.

Speaking of sacrifices, what's the difference between an inconvenience and a sacrifice? I will share with you a story that reflects it better than I ever could. There's this farmer named Jones who fell on hard times. The more he struggled to catch up with bills that came past due, the more he got behind. The weather wasn't cooperating at all and the crops withered and died in the fields due to lack of moisture. As the downturn deepened, Jones used up all his reserves. At about this same time, the animals in the barnyard noticed the predicament Farmer Jones was in. They gathered together to discuss how they could help Farmer Jones because he always took care of them so well.

They wondered to each other as to what they could do to help. The chicken thought and spoke up first, "Hey, I could lay some more eggs for Farmer Jones to take and sell in town. He's been real good to me and that's the least I could do to help." All the other animals agreed that this was a good idea. Then the cow spoke up next, "You know what? I could have a calf and then the farmer would have some milk to sell to make some more money." Another great idea they all thought. Next, the sheep stepped forward and spoke, "Hey, I've been listening to all of you and I was thinking he might as well shave off this wool coat of mine and sell it. It's been pretty warm out lately and I don't need it anymore." They all came up with great ways to help out Farmer Jones except for one animal.

All the other animals turned in unison to look at the pig as he sheepishly started backing away from the other animals. The pig knew his turn was coming because every one of the animals came up with ways to help the farmer out of his financial bind, but what could he do? As the rest of the farm animals looked on and waited for his reply as to how he was going to help the farmer out, he looked at them and said, "This isn't fair because you're only *inconvenienced* while helping Farmer Jones. What you're asking of me is a real *sacrifice*. I have to give my life in order to be able to help him out because all I have to give is bacon and ham."

This story sums up the difference between an inconvenience and a sacrifice. There are many times in our lives where we'll be inconvenienced on the road of spiritual enlightenment, but there'll probably be a few times when we'll be asked to make a sacrifice. Maybe that will be giving up a dream you've had since childhood or giving up a career you've fought hard to achieve. It could include giving up certain family members who just aren't able to see and bless your new way of living. It may also mean giving up your life in a sense.

One thing I've found though through personal experience is when I've been willing to make a sacrifice it didn't necessarily mean I would have to make the sacrifice in the end. It's my willingness to let go and make the sacrifice that's the actual demonstration of my faith. Whatever each of us is asked to sacrifice will be unique to each and every one of us.

A Journey of Remembering

CHAPTER 12: YEARNING FOR LEARNING

Life is what happens when you reach that jumping off place.

By this time on your spiritual path, you'll be experiencing a new life. Embrace it, experience it, and love it, because you've created it in concert with God. That's why you've acted in concert with God, so that God may experience Himself experientially.

We now have the beginning of a wonderfully new and loving relationship with our Creator. Now we need to help it to grow and expand. How do we do that? We need to know more. There are many people who inquire about spiritual matters, but very few have enough patience to wait for the answers and even fewer apply it once the answers do come.

After my spiritual awakening I experienced a great yearning, for what I didn't know. The feeling was way down deep inside, it was like a burning fire. All I knew was I couldn't shut it off even if I wanted to. I guess it came down to an extreme "yearning for learning." I couldn't get enough! I wanted to know everything there was to know about love, life, and God. Looking back now, I would say I not only wanted to know these things, but I wanted to experience them both physically and spiritually. I was taught before that all I needed to know about God was He was all-powerful and He's to be feared. With my new relationship with Life, that type of thinking wasn't going to work for me anymore.

I thought it was just plain wrong to view God that way. I knew

A Journey of Remembering

He wasn't to be feared, and there had to be some way to see God as being more than just all-powerful. It seemed like God was being put into a box by limiting Him and what He is; it seemed to limit His essence. So I asked myself these questions: Does God have a sense of humor? How compassionate is He? Does He have fun? Does He experience joy? Does He experience sadness? Is He a He or a She, or neither, or both? Is there really a Devil or was this man-made? What's God's plan? How do I fit into that greater plan? Why was I asking these questions when not too many other people were? Was I totally crazy?

As I've discussed earlier, I felt maybe I should go to the source for the answers. I tried talking to other people about these things but for the most part I got some really weird looks cast my way for even putting these questions into word form. "You don't question things like that, and you surely don't question God about them," was what I was told by most people I asked. To be quite honest, that worked for a while; I caved in and didn't question things.

I did just what the popular beer commercials wanted me to do. One commercial of the 90's was this: "Why ask why? It's it and that's that." No further investigation was needed as they saw it. We've been taught our whole lives not to question things. We get this indoctrination of not questioning things from government (which rarely likes questions about the things they're up to) to religion (which absolutely forbids questioning anything about their beliefs or dogma) to our parents (who after a while hate the words "Why?" and "How come?"), and finally, the educational system.

Don't be surprised if this takes a while to undo as we've assimilated much misleading information over the years, in fact we're still bombarded with it every day. For myself, I ask this question when I doubt someone else's assessment of something: Does this work for me? If the answer is no, then I'm off on another journey to find something that will work.

Once I've pondered a question or a certain position, I *have* to find an answer. Do you think (use a little common sense here) God created us *not* to question things? Wouldn't we just be a bunch of sheep being pushed around? Are we to just take someone else's view of something and then call it good, call it our own? This is where we've really screwed up. We've chosen to accept the so-called truths of our parents, religion, government, and most of all our fellow man, as the only way it could possibly be. By choosing to accept their truths, we've chosen to accept their experience and make it our own, even if it goes totally contrary to what we're feeling inside at the time.

When we go contrary to those feelings inside, it's at this time the longings of the soul are denied. With this denial, we embark on a journey that will take us a long way off the path of our soul's enlightenment. The soul is on a mission of personal enlightenment, not enlightenment because of someone else's experience. It's now time to put an end to this type of enlightenment because it's not true enlightenment at all. True enlightenment comes from the episodes of life the soul has personally chosen to experience.

For instance, if you choose to have the experience of compassion (you do this by not taking someone else's word for it, but by living it) then you need to open up and allow yourself to be there. Where's there? There is a state of being; it's not something you do, it's a state of *beingness*. When you're being truly compassionate, there's no thinking about how you're going to get there because you're already there; you're in a state of being called compassion. When you're in that state of being, the results are instantaneous; there's no thinking beforehand on *how* to be compassionate, you just are. This is a shortcut to creation; a shortcut from and to God and the results are immediate.

By the time you've reached this state of being, the soul has evolved very much. In order to be truly compassionate, you'll have needed to have experienced the opposite of compassion, which is a lack of love on your part. In other words, you'll need to have experienced a type of hell. To have true compassion for someone else's situation, it helps tremendously to have been in their shoes at one time or another.

Here's an example of this: You know true compassion for someone who's lost a child in a car accident or through disease because you've been through the same thing. It doesn't necessarily have to be an identical situation, but close enough to identify. You can identify with the feelings of guilt, anger, loss, or the other emotions of grief. You can identify with those feelings because you've experienced them yourself through the loss of your own child or other loved one. It's through these types of experiences we become a part *of* others, not a part *from* them.

Can you see where we're going with this? We're sharing a commonality and that commonality is the presence of God. This is when true healing experiences happen. Does it not say in the Bible "For where two or three come together in my name, there am I with them?" (Matthew 18:20). God never was, or ever will be, because He's in a constant state of being, a *being* of now. Therefore the words, "I AM THAT I AM" (Exodus 3:14).

Other types of beingness are many. Some of the positive states of beingness are: loving, kind, humble, trustworthy, showing empathy and sympathy while being nonjudgmental and open-minded, along with joyful and happy; the list can go on and on. States of being can be of the negative sense as well. These may include sadness, anger, frustration, and others like these. These are all states of being our souls choose to experience. If you're being the first one I listed (which is love), then you'll have found another shortcut to enlightenment. When someone is being love, they are automatically being all the other positive states of being. Love is compassionate, sympathetic, unbiased, fearfree, joyful, and happy. Love is all these things rolled into one. Having found this unconditional love, you'll have truly *experienced* God first hand.

A Journey of Remembering

CHAPTER 13: PARAMETERS OF GOD

*"Freedom is just another word for nothing left to lose." -
Janis Joplin*

When someone poses a question, they've put the powers of creation into action to bring them the answer. The powers of the universe are set into motion in order to fulfill a desire to know, and to truly know something, one must experience it. Did He not say: "Ask and it will be given; knock and it shall be opened?" (Luke 11:9). God doesn't mind being used by us because He puts Himself at our disposal to be used for the purpose of soul enlightenment.

This is how the soul begins the creation of these experiences. Within the parameters that are set up, desiring something brings it into the realm of usefulness. I use the word parameter here because it better defines what God has in mind for us. According to the dictionary, parameter means: *a basic factor in determining the nature of a system.* God's parameters include the freedom to do as we need to do, within certain boundaries. An example of this would be expecting to somehow become a doctor by going to an electrical engineering school. One has to be within the parameters of medical school (not electrical engineering) to become a licensed doctor; so medical school is the basic factor that determines the nature of the system in becoming a doctor.

Parameters are set up for not only physical existence, but also for the spiritual world. Let's take the law of gravity; we can't exist here in human form without it. We may not like the consequences of gravity sometimes, but we learn to live with it and we learn to use it. It's the same while using the parameters of the spirit world. We learn to live within them and in the process, we become conscious of them. I say conscious of them, because we've been *unconsciously* using them all the time to our own detriment.

Jesus used these powers many times; He lived within them. Did Jesus not say that we would do these same works He did and many more? (John 14:12). Jesus availed himself of these powers and we're meant to do the same. That's why He came here, to give us many examples of how it's done. Each day, more people are becoming aware of these powers that have always been here. We can't be aware and use them though if we only continue to see the material or physical world as separate from the spiritual world. We need to develop a spiritual sense of sorts, and this takes a little practice and open-mindedness.

We're now going to explore some of these parameters that both the physical and spiritual world have in common. The first parameter we're going to look at is the act of wanting something. If you look up the word *want* you'll find it to mean: *to be without, or a lack of*. Quite apparently when you want something, you're expressing to the universe that you're lacking something. When you say, "I want this or that," you've just created that very thing in your reality; a desire which is expressed through a feeling of not having a particular this or that. Within the parameters God's put into place, you'll receive *exactly* what you're feeling or stating.

The words "I am ..." or "I ..." are the greatest creative forces known to humans because when you use those words, you've engaged the powers of life, so be careful when making a statement of wanting something. When you state you want to go back to school for more education, that's exactly what you'll receive, more *feelings* of wanting to go to school; not the actual feelings of being a student in school. Can you see the negative connotation wanting is? Can you now see how the creative forces at you're disposal work for everyone and everything? You have to quit wanting things in order to get them. Here's a shortcut to attain your desired goals: Just claim them out loud and let life bring it to you. Don't say, "I want to go to school." Say,

"I'm going to school." It's really that simple; you just have to stay focused on your goal.

When you quit the beingness of wanting, then you'll finally get what you've been after. You need to quit the act of wanting and start *the act of having*. In my own case, I wanted the experience of staying sober, but the more I wanted it, the harder it was to achieve. I was caught up in the circular act of always wanting. You see, wanting is not having. If you're in a state of being called having, there are no wants. All things have already been provided for.

Spirituality requires action on your part, positive action. I use the words *positive* or *negative* in the manner of either taking you towards enlightenment or holding you back from it. They're not used in the normal sense of "rightness" or "wrongness." They're used in a sense of beingness. For myself, I needed to get off my ass and start *being* sober. We create something by being it. This is a short cut around the creating that is done by thought, word, and deed. This is another of the parameters that crosses over into the physical world.

By being in spiritual consciousness, you create much faster in the physical world, instantaneous in fact. Creating by thought, word, and deed takes what we call time. In the spirit realm there's no such thing as time because the spirit realm is always in a constant state of beingness. It takes no time to *be* in a spiritual sense because you're already there. Understand? That's the way it works: If you're seeking a higher level of enlightenment, then quit wanting it, skip the doing parts, and just be it.

Did you notice I said to skip the doing? Doing is also a process of sorts; it's like the wanting thing. There's a big difference between *doing* something and *being* something. Doing is being stuck in the action of not arriving, not achieving. Being something on the other hand is the action of not only arriving and achieving, it's a state of divine existence. This is truly experiencing Life in all its glory. Can you see how this always brings us back to God? So did we ever leave? No, we just forgot. We need to remember as in re-member (or re-assemble) something, as in "putting it all back together." What we've always been seeking is to get back together with God. That is the yearning of the soul: to feel at home (even when we're not there).

A Journey of Remembering

As to re-membering, what humans need to do is quit the action of learning. We just need to re-member. We need to remember what our soul's desire was in the first place. We should be calling our present educational system outmoded and update it with an experiencing and remembering system. How much input did you have in the learning process while you were growing up? From my point of view, I was railroaded into the believe system I grew up with. I knew bodily harm would come to me if I were to even question some of the things I was being taught. This is not free will; this is coercion of the worst kind!

I want to share one small example of this from my childhood. Remember in the early years of grade school when we are supposed to stand and say the *Pledge of Allegiance* to the flag in the morning? Well, because of my religious beliefs, I wasn't to stand and pledge allegiance to the flag. While every one of my classmates stood up to say the Pledge of Allegiance, I was to remain seated and say nothing. I was not given a choice in the matter; either I sat and kept silent or I'd be beaten when I got home!

According to my religion, I was not to be any part of the so-called outside world. My religion and parents made it extremely clear to me if I did salute the flag, then I would be worshiping *it*, instead of *God*, which is really wrong! But yet, that didn't seem right to me. We lived in the freest country on the planet. This country was formed by men and women who longed for religious freedom, in fact millions died to make it happen. My own father fought in World War II to keep this country free. It just didn't make any sense to me. We had the freedom to practice this religion because of the very world I was not to be a part of. How was I going to make any sense of these mixed messages I was being given? I couldn't.

Well I'll tell you what, it took five years of daily humiliation before I made my stand, and I mean that literally. I'm here to tell you that sitting there day-after-day, month-after-month, and year-after-year was one of the most humiliating experiences of my entire life. Every school day morning, everyone stood up to say the Pledge of Allegiance and there I sat looking down into my hands, totally ashamed of myself. I remained seated because I was so afraid of what my old man or God would do to me. I *knew* I would surely be smitten on the spot if I stood up and put my hand on my heart and said the Pledge of Allegiance. That day, ten-year-old Nathan made his Great Stand! I said, "Screw it! I've had enough of this shit!" (Yes, even then I had a potty mouth. I even had a note attached to my report card I had to show to my parents. That one was good for a motherly hour-long lecture from the Bible). As the teacher told all the students to stand for the pledge, I struggled to stand upright on trembling legs. As I proceeded to say the Pledge of Allegiance right along side everyone else, a dead silence enveloped the room. We all stood in shock and disbelief, wondering what to do next. It wasn't until the teacher came to her senses and started the reciting of the pledge that the spell was broken.

I finally had enough of being the laughing stock every morning. It was my single greatest act of defiance. I wasn't going to be squashed into their (my parents and my religions) mold anymore! Believe me when I say I was willing to suffer the punishment for my defiance. Really, it couldn't have been any worse than what I'd been through every morning for years while I just sat there in total humiliation.

With that very simple act of defiance, I earned my rebel wings and I've been damned proud of them ever since. I never suffered from the punishment I so gravely feared because my parents never found out about it. God surely knew about it, yet He didn't strike me down. I guess in looking back at it now, I had followed in the Ultimate Rebel's footsteps. I made my stand, just as Jesus did. In a sense and at a later time though, I would be put to death for my "rebelness" (I had to make this word up because it's not in the dictionary even though it's awful close to rebelliousness). Today I thank God for that whole experience because this is when I found my true freedom and calling. Later on, I was to experience the ultimate form of unconditional love.

CHAPTER 14: BEINGNESS

Accept nothing at face value! Question everything!

This is one of the single, greatest pieces of advice I've ever received from anyone, *Accept nothing at face value. Question everything!* That should include everything you've ever been told, taught, experienced, or felt. Keep this in mind as you embark on this journey of discovery as to the true nature of life in all its glory. Are you ready? If your mind is closed off, now would be a good time to ask for an open one. You *will* receive it! One quick note on questioning: Just because we question something makes it neither good nor bad. It's our relationship to the answer or our perspective of the answer, that we then deem them to be either good or bad.

It's only through your experiences you'll be able to tell if something is right for you. It all lies in your perspective of the answer. Does it fit into how you want to see yourself now? Do these things fit into how you want to create yourself? Is it your Highest Truth? How can you expand on this new relationship with Life, Love, and God if you don't question whether the present one is working for you?

By obtaining answers to questions like I've previously posed, you begin to define yourself. When you define yourself, you define God. How can that be? By assuming that what you've been taught over the years is the gospel truth, you've come to accept the fact that there can be no other way of seeing it. While doing this you've limited your knowledge and experience of God. Many people have been taught God is to be feared, and He's a vengeful and punishing God. Many take these teachings at face value and seek no further, and through this very process they've created just that, a nasty God who's to be feared. No matter where they look, they'll see God's heavy hand because this is what their thinking is based on. Here is where questioning comes in. What if He's not a vengeful God? What if He's nothing but pure love and can't be anything else?

By just asking questions like these, you've quit assuming your previous knowledge is right for you and your mind has begun to open. It's begun to open to other avenues or ideas, and maybe one of these other avenues might be the one called common sense. By the way, do you know why it's call *common* sense? Because it's common to each and every one of us, we all have it; it's that little voice inside of you, directing and guiding you.

So, let's use a little common sense on this next problem. God has given us free will; that much we can all pretty well agree on. It's said we're given the freedom to choose between good and evil. If we choose well then we go to heaven, but if we choose evil (or less than perfection), then it's off to Hell. Once in Hell, we burn and are tortured for eternity. Is this really free will? It sounds more like coercion to me because if we choose wrong, then its eternal damnation. Pardon the pun, but what the hell is this?

It's not free will if part of the equation holds coercion and punishment. We would be choosing (or forced) to do good simply because we don't want to see the wrath of God, so that makes it forced will. It's as if God were saying to us, "You have to do it this way or else!" Once again, this is forced will. There's a big difference between *choosing* a way because it's the way you want to go, and choosing a way because it's the way you're being *forced* to go.

I have an example of this for you. Let's say you're driving down the road and you come to a "T" in the road. You have the choice to either turn right or left, but upon arriving there you notice the road going to the left has a baracade in front of it which says there's road construction ahead and the bridge is out. Now common sense says not to go that way because you could end up in big trouble. So is this really a choice as to which way you can go? No, because you have no choice; you're forced to take the road to the right. A *true* free-will choice would have been when you approached the "T" in the road you could've chosen to go either way and still arrive at your destination.

Think on this for a minute: Do you not steal a bicycle because you might get caught and punished, or do you choose not to steal a bike because that's not who you are or who you choose to be? Can you see the difference? I believe God gave us total free will to choose to do what works well because that's who we are or who we choose to be, not who we're forced to be.

Who wants to be loved because we've been forcing them to love us? Not I, because that's not love. True love is unconditional, no strings attached (and I mean *no* strings). There's no greater joy than to be loved for just who you are right now, and that my friend is how God loves you. He loves you unconditionally. You don't have to fear Him because you're not going to be punished in hell for not loving Him just the right way. You may even exercise the option of denying His existence, but no matter, He still loves you. We're all welcomed home with open arms surrounded by unconditional love.

Speaking of punishment, what's the difference between punishment and consequences? First off, there's no such thing as good punishment. Punishment was invented by *men* to force a set of behaviors they deemed good onto someone else. Punishment always involves some kind of pain, whether it's emotional, physical, or spiritual. Contrary to what the Bible says, God can't inflict painful punishment on people because He is love; it's not in His nature. God can't be something He's not. Only man does that!

Let's examine what consequences really are. Consequences are the natural outcomes of the choices we make or made in the past; it's real simple. Consequences know neither good nor bad; they just are what they are. Consequences result from an action set into motion which results in a positive or negative outcome. A consequence of throwing a ball is it's going to come down somewhere at some time. A consequence for driving too fast on an ice-covered road is you're going to crash. A consequence doesn't care if you're black or white, male or female, old or young; the parameters of consequence apply equally to all. I call this the "Consequential Theory of Life." This is what is meant when it says in the Bible "the rain falls on the just and the unjust" (Matthew 5:45).

Yes, God did make some laws or parameters in which we live; He had to. They are natural laws. If we didn't have these parameters, we couldn't be here, for there would be total and utter chaos. What some may see as punishment from God is in reality a consequence of some natural law or parameter being broken. Most of the parameters that are in force for us humans deal with the mind because thought is first creator. Our thinking is what gets us into trouble, not God.

Many of us have been using the process of thinking and creating unconsciously. We need to think in a different way (consciously), one that will get us our desired results. We can't think God is one way and then act a different way. We can't think God is Love, if all we see Him doing is punishing us for doing wrong. The laws of God progress in a natural and orderly way. They are what they are. They are common sense.

We need to understand these parameters if we're to truly know and experience God. Here's another way to look at it. Before you can do anything, you must first have the thought about it. Let's use this example: "I need a drink of water." This is a thought or a feeling expressed. It's a thought of a supposed need. As long as you keep thinking it, that's exactly what you'll continue to experience; a wanting (or feeling) for a drink of water. If you progress with this thought, then you express it like this, "I need a drink of water, I'm thirsty." That's great, but guess what? You're still thirsty. The next step in this progression requires action. You have to physically demonstrate the need by getting up off the chair, walk across the room, find a glass, fill it with water, and drink it. Now it is no longer a need or a want. You're now *experiencing* the feeling of not being thirsty or in other words, *unthirstyness*, or the state of being of not being thirsty anymore. So to sum this thirsty thing up, it goes like this: Thought, word, and deed equal a state of being!

I know I've mentioned this before, but it's worth repeating. There's a shortcut for creating states of beingness. Skip the word and deeds in the action and just not be thirsty. When in a true state of being, one does not think about how to do it, you just find yourself there. You don't think every step of the process out, you just find yourself with a glass of water in your hand, drinking it. States of being require no conscious thought before hand. You just find yourself at where you're at.

A Journey of Remembering

No matter which way you do it, you are expressing your desires. You are exercising your free will. There's no punishment for not taking the drink of water, only consequences. One of the consequences for not taking the drink is still having the feeling of being thirsty. There's another consequence (a positive one) here though. When you've taken the drink of water, you're experiencing the feeling of unthirstyness or that state of being, and guess what just happened? Not only are you in a new state of being, you've found yet another state of being, the freedom from want! All this from just wanting to wet your whistle! Pretty cool, huh? These parameters apply equally to the action of being thirsty to quitting smoking to being an astronaut! It doesn't matter what the desire is, it always works the same for everyone.

What I'm talking about here is *real* freedom. When you have this type of freedom, you're engaging the forces of the universe to bring you more of the same. So hang onto your hat and I mean that. You'll no longer have to *work* for success (by success I mean spiritual success), and since all things are spiritual in nature, it means success in *all areas* of your life. God will bring it to you! This can apply to anything in your life. All things are spiritual in nature. I used this example of thirst to try and simplify a really complex idea, but it could apply to anything you are going through. It could include a divorce, a career change, maybe the birth of a child or some other personal issue you have to deal with. Use it and I guarantee it'll work.

Now, can you see how you've been using these forces all of your life? At least for me, it hasn't necessarily been for the advancement of my enlightenment, unless it has. We need to make conscious effort to effect changes in how we use these forces. God's given us such valuable tools to use and we've been using them to our detriment. We need to remember how to use them for our advancement, not our hindrance.

You're not a product of your creation; your creation is a product of you. What you create is how you want to show yourself and your state of being. Now do you see why the world in general is in so much trouble? We've been putting the cart before the horse. We've been trying to push the cart instead of leading the cart. Everyone knows it's much easier to steer something when you're pulling it. That is both a spiritual parameter and a physical law. Cars which are front wheel driven are much less likely to spin out of control than rear wheel driven cars because it's much more natural (physics laws apply here) to pull something than it is to push it. Something that's pushed will tend to want to remain going in a straight line. And when this happens, you're going against the natural forces if you want to turn, but pull something along and it will naturally want to follow in the steered path.

So apply these laws or parameters to your own spiritual growth; pull, don't push. Be the creation of your product (or spirituality), not a product of your creation. Lead; don't follow because when you follow you're always playing catch-up. Be in the forefront of God's creation, because this is what God would have us be. Remember this: When pulling something or being in the forefront, it's much easier to remain flexible to unforeseen circumstances. By the way, there should be no unforeseen circumstances because you're now in the front where you can see what you're creating and how you'll need to bend or twist to fit the circumstances.

When you're in the rear pushing something, this is when *unforeseen* things happen because it's very hard to see what's happening. No wonder we run into so many things in our lives, when if only we could have seen better! Another quick note on this cart thing (these ideas just keep coming, so I keep writing), when you're in the front of the cart, you're *being a leader*, but when you're in the rear, you're *being a follower*. Which would you rather *be*?

This is *your* choice as to how much freedom you have in your life. This freedom was God given to each of us when came here. Now you should be able to more clearly understand it when I say you'll remain a victim until you're not. We're victims of our *own* circumstances. We created the circumstances by our own creation process (thought, word, action). *We* created it. We remain in these conditions as being held hostage, until we create the circumstances differently. God gave us that power to change things. Are you going to use them this time for your advancement?

Do you know someone who always seems to have a major

crisis going on in their life? I know quite a few personally. It seems no sooner do they extradite themselves from one crisis, than it's into the next one. They never seem to tire of it. Oh, they may say they're tired of it, but yet the actions don't match the words. I think they actually love the drama of it all. Since I've become an observer, I've learned the true meaning of the saying: "Your actions are speaking so loud I can't hear what you're saying."

This brings me to another great piece of advice that has been shared with me. *Be* an observer. Don't try to observe, or want to be an observer, just *be an observer*. By observer, I mean someone who takes notes of things, or watches. Take note of other's words and actions. Take note of your own words and actions. Do they match? They'll tell you much about where you and your actions are and what you're trying to accomplish in your souls' journeys. You can gain much experience by closely observing the actions or creations of others and yourself. One of the greatest observations I've witnessed myself is as long as the action is repeated over and over again, the results will be exactly the same, over and over again. That can go either way for so-called good results or bad ones.

Let's look at an example of this from my own personal archives. The more I wanted to get sober, the more it eluded me. Each time I drank I would tell myself this time it will be different; I won't get sick and puke my guts out and make a jackass out of myself or get into trouble with the law, yet each time the results were the same. I would get sick and I wouldn't behave myself. This is insanity. I repeated the same behavior (getting drunk) over and over again, yet I expected different results each time. The parameters of God can't be broken. They have to be perfect each and every time. How can He make it so some people can get away with breaking them at times, while others may not? He can't because then it wouldn't be fair to anyone.

Now, let's take this the other way. Each day I wake up and have a little quiet time for God and myself. I tell myself and God I'm powerless over alcohol, I can't do this on my own, and I require His help. This time I'm repeating the same behavior over and over again (just like before in my drinking career), and I'm getting the exact same result of that action over and over again, with much better results though. I'm *being* sober over and over. Did you notice I didn't say I *wanted* to be sober? Or *maybe* God can help me? My little prayer is a *statement* of who I am, and when I make statements of whom I am, than that's who I am. These are some of the greatest prayers you can ever pray. We create our conditions and ourselves every moment of every day.

I also thank Him for the day of life and the blessings He's sending my way. I thank Him for blessing my home and all who enter it or bless those I may come into contact with throughout the day, and that's *exactly* what happens. He blesses all I encounter in my day as my soul goes journeying along. I take God along for the ride, and what a ride it's been.

You know, I still have occasional rough days. Sometimes things just don't fall into place like I've grown accustomed to for some time now. Is it the end of the world when things don't go so nicely? No way, I appreciate those days as well. Those off days are part of the total perfection of the journey. It also helps me in the fact I need to keep on top of this spiritual life; to keep on *being* a being. The minute I stop being is the moment I go stagnant, and that's when I miss seeing the perfection of it all. The minute I quit being, I miss out on all the miracles that go on minute-to-minute in my life and in yours. This "miracling" is what we are going to explore in the next chapter on miracles.

CHAPTER 15: MIRACLES

"Miracles are propitious accidents, the natural causes of which are too complicated to be readily understood."-
George Santayana

Now we're going to take a stab at understanding what miracles are and how they happen. First off, here's the definition of a miracle according to Webster's Dictionary: *a **wonderful** thing; or an act or happening attributed to a supernatural power; a **wonder***. Are miracles an accident? No. Nothing happens in God's (and our) plan by accident. There's no such thing as a coincidence and there's no such thing as fate. The day you quit believing in these things will be the day you see and experience miracles all over the place, all of the time.

Early on in my spiritual quest for understanding (after I sobered up) two friends and I decided to take a trip out to the western U.S. We called it the Great Drunken Sojourn of '92. By the way, we didn't get drunk nor did we plan on it, we just like to have fun with our sobriety. It was really a spiritual quest of sorts. I was sober a little over a year then and this was kind of a little celebration of that. Anyway, we had no set timetable for the journey. We figured on being gone for a few weeks. We were going to take in the sites and see all the National Parks from Yellow Stone to Glacier with a stop at the Redwoods in California. After the redwoods we would sweep southeast and see a few more parks on the way home.

Since we didn't have any real plans to speak of, things could change at a moment's notice without us much caring about it. If we didn't feel like seeing something, then we'd skip it and move on. Maybe we'd stay a little longer at the next stop, we didn't know and didn't really care; we were just going with the flow of things. We were

A Journey of Remembering

going to have a relaxing vacation and just enjoy ourselves. We'd find a phone booth (this was before cell phones were around) and call home every few days to let loved ones know we were okay and how things were going. The trip was progressing like trips usually do; sometimes you have an unfortunate circumstance or two along the way. I've got to tell you about a couple of them!

As you probably know, three men on a trip don't take the necessary time and effort to plan things too well. One of things we never did was to pack a lunch for the long car rides. We just ate whatever was handy as we journeyed forth. You know the routine; a bag of chips here, couple of sodas there, maybe throw in a couple of candy bars to make it a complete meal. When we reached our campsite for the night, we'd make a good supper and hit the hay. As we approached the Rockies on the way to Yellowstone, my stomach started growling. I dug around the car looking for something to eat. I came across a fresh bag of red licorice that looked pretty enticing, so I had some. The problem was I didn't quit with just some; I damn near ate the whole one-pound bag myself and I'm not that big of a person (body wise).

As we reached the end of a very long day of traveling, we found ourselves in the Rockies looking for a suitable campsite. We wearily set up camp, planning to fix supper and then get some much needed rest. We were able to find a comfortable site, which wasn't hard to do because the trip took place early in the spring with the summer rush of tourism still a few weeks off. As we were setting up camp, my stomach started to emit some rather ominous sounds. Noticing the sounds coupled with not feeling well at the time, I skipped supper and headed straight for the comfort and protection of the sturdy tent and my warm sleeping bag. I figured it was too long a day and I was overtired. I fell fast asleep for a short time only to be wakened by an intense stomachache that it would've made an elephant tear up. When I get that bad a stomachache, I know what's happening next.

I'll tell you what; I couldn't get out of that sleeping bag fast enough! I knew where the outdoor privy was and I was heading in the right direction. About halfway there it dawned on me that I wasn't

A Journey of Remembering

going to make it. I had to shit, and now! Oh God, what a sight I must have been! The temperature is only fifteen degrees. It's pitch black and snowing moderately, and here I am, pants down around my ankles, taking a massive dump right in the middle of someone else's campsite! Yep, I was on a real spiritual journey here! I finished my business and returned to the comfort of my warm sleeping bag. I felt better and on the upswing after the little trip over to the neighbor's campsite.

What's the moral of this story? Don't eat that much licorice on an empty stomach while riding in a car for a long duration; it's just like drinking a gallon of castor oil. That stuff will set you free and clean you out. So, where's the miracle in this, you ask? Hell, it was a miracle I made it as far as I did before loosing that load. Sometimes you just have to find the humor in things. I'm sorry, but looking back now, I think this was the funniest parts of the whole trip. I'm still laughing about it and of course so are my buddies! Oh well.

As dawn was breaking over the mountaintops, we hastily tore the tent down because it smelled like we'd set up camp next to a sewage treatment plant. We set our sights on Glacier Park in Montana. As we checked into the ranger station and were assigned a campsite, they informed us some of the higher passes were still closed as they hadn't quite finished plowing the snow out yet. After pitching the tent in a much better smelling surrounding, we decided to see how far up the mountain we could drive, appreciative of the fact we could only go so far. About three-quarters of the way up the mountain and on the righthand side was a little spot where you could pull over and park while taking pictures or do some stretching while getting out the body kinks. This was almost as far as we could go anyway because just ahead around the next switchback is where the road was closed due to the deep winter snow pack.

After pulling over, my buddy Dale (who was driving) gets out and stretches while looking around. I was sitting in the middle of the back seat while my other friend Terry was sitting up front in the passenger's seat. I fumbled around looking for my camera to take some photos and after finding some film, exited the car. I stepped out and walked around to the back of the car and did some stretching myself just as Terry was getting out. We all seemed to hear it at the

A Journey of Remembering

same time. Time slowed dramatically as everything went into slow motion. There was a deep rumbling sound from the mountainside off to our right and up above us. The three of us looked around and then all our eyes locked on each other at the same time. We all yelled in unison, "Holy shit, it's a rock slide!"

I took off like an Olympic athlete in the 100-meter sprint. Dale took off straight from the driver's side heading across the road which included a thousand foot drop-off. Terry seemed to sprout wings and off he flew in the same direction the car was pointed (I haven't seen that man move that fast before or since). I hadn't run far when I stopped and turned around to see what was coming off the cliff's face from up above. About eighty feet up, here came a couple of little pebbles closely pursued by a rolling fifty-pound rock. As I sized it up from my vantage point, I could tell the arc and distance was going to be perfect. I could see there was no way this rock was going to miss the car. Sure enough, down it came and slashed through the car's roof as its momentum carried it downward into the back seat while landing in the exact place I had been sitting just a few seconds before. It landed with such a fury that it knocked all the dirt and rust off on the underside of the car. I half expected it to continue its journey all the way through the seat and floorboard, but it stopped short with a muddled thud.

We stood there in stunned silence for a minute while waiting for any leftovers to come down. We cautiously approached the car to see how much damage was done. Upon inspection, it looked like someone used a can opener on the roof. The rock had left an almost perfect rectangular hole that measured eight inches wide and twenty inches long. About this time my whole body started shaking violently and I couldn't make it quit. *Now* I was scared! That was a little too close for me. I didn't know what the hell was going on; the night before, I'm shitting my guts out and now I'm having rocks thrown at me. This was getting to be one hell of spiritual quest!

There was nothing left to do but get the duct tape out (yes, we're all rednecks) and patch the hole. We got back in the car and headed for the ranger station to report what happened. Upon arriving there, a real nice ranger lady recorded our names and addresses, car information, and everything that happened. We were about to leave after showing her the rock and the damage to the car roof when I held up the rock and said, "I know we're not allowed to remove anything from the park, but this rock is going home with me to be part of a fireplace in my cabin someday." She laughed and with a little twinkle in her eye said, "I think we can allow it this time."

    The three of us figured we'd seen enough excitement for one day and headed back to the comfort of our campsite. Supper was made and we sat around the fire for a while discussing what happened earlier in the day. It soon grew dark and we hit the hay dreaming of a better tomorrow.

    The next day dawned bright and sunny with a chill in the air. Not one to be knocked back for too long, we set out to finish the trip up the mountain and settle in at the top for some quiet time. Everything went much better this time. I took a lot of photos of the mountains and the indescribable scenery. God sure showed His handywork when He created that chunk of real estate. It almost felt like heaven up there. It was so peaceful and quiet, a beautiful spot for some one-on-one communication with Life. We stayed for about an hour and then headed down. As we were coming down the mountain (heading back to the campsite for some dinner and packing up) we passed a park ranger's Jeep headed in the opposite direction.

    As soon as he passed us, he turned his red lights on while whipping his car around in the middle of the road. Always one to keep an eye peeled for cops (an old behavior that hadn't quite left me yet) I yelled to Dale we had a park ranger on our ass and he was going to pull us over. Now what!? I knew Dale wasn't speeding (he never did), so why was he pulling us over? He approached the car as Dale rolled down his window. "Are you Dale V.?" he asked. Dale replied, "Yep, that's me." The ranger replied the reason he pulled us over was they'd received a bulletin to be on a lookout for the three of us. We were wanted men! An APB (All Points Bulletin) was passed out to all the western National Parks to keep an eye out for us. Dale's wife had it issued because his father had passed away and they needed him back home immediately. The ranger remarked they never would've found us if we hadn't reported the rock coming through our car roof the day

A Journey of Remembering

before! To finish the story quickly, we packed up and drove nearly 24 hours straight through to get back in time to help with the funeral and be with the loved ones. What a trip.

Now, it doesn't take a rocket scientist to see what the miracle is here, or I should say miracles. Nobody had a clue where we were at because it had been a few days since we last called home. We could've been anywhere in those western fifteen states. Needless to say, I was taken aback. This was some heavy stuff. I was now standing in the presence of greatness! What seemed as a chunk of bad luck because of the rock coming through the car roof, actually turned out to be a message sent straight from the Big Guy. *I'm here to tell you, when God needs to get your attention, sometimes He throws rocks at you!* (That's meant to be humorous). In spite of the news we'd just been handed, we all had a good laugh at that one.

I think this is a great spot to stop and ponder something. Read it slowly and think about it carefully: *Either God is or He isn't. If He is, then either He is everything or He is nothing. If He is everything, then let Him be everything. If He is nothing, then He is still something, because nothing is still something.*

Ponder and wonder about these truths I've just written. There are no half-measures in spirituality and there are no half-truths. It's either all or nothing; there's no in-between. In-between measures, attitudes, and ideas have gotten the human race into a world of trouble and this is where they'll keep us. You need to make a stand on this, because this one single thing is determining the whole course and evolution of our souls and the world at large.

Up to the time of our '92 Drunken Sojourn, I was advised it would be extremely helpful to me if I quit believing in accidents or coincidences (for either God is or He isn't). Needless to say, I was having a hard time doing it because that's what I came to believe throughout my whole life up until this time. I was taught we have free will, but we're victims of accidents and fate. In a way, I felt we were just along for the ride. It's hard for a person to change his thinking that much overnight, you know? But a person would have to be blind in a sense *not* to see this as a miracle and there were major forces at work here. Guess what? I changed my mind overnight, at least when it came

A Journey of Remembering

to big coincidences and accidents like this one.

Could it really be true that everything that happens in our lives is for an ultimate or greater purpose? Asking myself that question really made me stop and think. I had to look back at all those seeming coincidences and accidents that happened in my life up until that time and question myself if maybe there isn't some bigger Plan involved here. Being pretty good at pondering things, there was no denying the events which happened in those two days were not just mere coincidences. I realized in a moment that my spiritual quest to the mountaintops had been successful after all.

By going on the spiritual quest with a closed mind though, I could've missed it all and just saw it as an ill-fated vacation of sorts. By closed mind, I mean having *preconceived* ideas as to how I *think* God should be working or acting in my life. If you think He's going to answer your prayers in a certain way, I'm pretty sure you'll be disappointed in the way they're answered for two reasons. The first reason you might be disappointed is you may have a preconceived idea He can only fix things in a certain way or time frame. When you do this, you are concentrating or focusing on seeing it only *one* way (the way *you* think God should fix it). While you're concentrating so hard on seeing it just one way, chances are you're going to miss the miracles because you're not looking in the right direction.

The second reason you may not like the outcome to your prayers is it may *appear* the prayer was never answered in the first place. Could that really be true? Are only certain prayers answered? I don't believe so. Once the soul has a longing, it can't be stopped; it will create what it desires. Sometimes this is where it gets a little tricky to see. We probably don't know what our soul's true short-term longings may be. The long-term goal is to experience everything we came here for. Where we are at on the time-line of enlightenment, only God knows.

To begin to be able to determine where we're at, we need at least two points of reference. Indulge me here for a minute because I'd like to demonstrate this. Find a pen or pencil and draw a four-inch line on a blank piece of paper. It doesn't matter if it's straight or crooked. Now, find the approximate middle and put a dot there. This shouldn't have been too hard to do because you have two points of reference to work from, the beginning and the end of the line. Now you'll have to use your imagination on the next part. Imagine a line in your head that extends forever in each direction; up and down or across, it doesn't matter. Now, find the middle of the line. You won't be able to because you have no point of reference to work off of; there's no start or ending point.

So while trying to determine what and how a prayer should be answered in the total time-line of the soul's enlightenment using our finite mind is impossible. The less in touch we are with God and our soul's course, the more in the dark we are and will remain. So what may *appear* to have not been answered, may already have been, or is yet to be answered. Then again, it may not even need to be answered because it's not the true longing of the soul at the time, it could just be a wanting of the finite mind as it tries to make sense of a difficult situation.

So it's in these ways we miss many of the miracles in our daily lives because we've so conditioned our mind to believe certain things only happen in certain ways or we have no reference points to work off of. This act is called assuming. And do you know what happens when you *assume*? You make an ass-of-u-and-me. *Ass-u-me*. See? So when we assume certain things about God or how God should be in our lives, it's at that moment we've closed off our minds to the other infinite possibilities he could use to help us along our way. When that happens, do you know what you get? You get a "God in a box." You'll have placed limits on Him (remember either He is everything or He is nothing?) and by doing that, how can you see or feel His many wondrous acts in your life?

Getting back to the rock through the car roof episode, think about this: God found us (though we were never lost, He knew where we were the whole time) and got a message to us (using material things) in only a few hours time when hardly a soul on earth knew where we were at. That is very humbling my friends. Now think about all the resources He put into motion to get that bulletin out to the right people. Think of how the bulletin happened to fall into just the right hands of the people who weren't even there the day before. They must

A Journey of Remembering

get many of these bulletins every day. What if we had been five minutes faster coming down the mountain, the ranger never would've seen us. Think of all the people's lives affected by this incident that didn't have a clue as to what was going on. When God has set a plan in motion, all one can do is stand back with mouth agape in wonder.

Here's something more to think about: The rock through the car roof escapade happened *before* his father passed away. Notice something here? God was not only in the *now* of things; He was in the *future and past* of things, so to speak. How can that be? Was it predestination that things happened the way they happened? No, I don't believe so, but we will talk more of this later on though.

In my mind, what happened was an impossiblilty; at least impossible for humans. How do you find three guys traveling in an old AMC Eagle in about 55 million people and who knows how many hundreds of thousands of square miles? Only an act of God could do something like that. If this happened to anyone else at the time, I would've said, "Why, that's a nifty coincidence" and left it at that just like I did many times before, but you see this happened to me. I was there and I experienced it. Being the doubting Thomas I was at the time, I can just hear God saying to the others with Him, "Stand back and watch this one. I'll get their attention now!"

Do you see how we're *all* part of God's plan even though ninety-five percent of us don't know it at the time? Can you see how very much we are interconnected to one another? Do you see now the meaning of Jesus' saying, "What you do onto the least of these my brother, you do onto me?" (Matthew 25:40). Jesus was trying to point out how truly inter-dependent and inter-connected we all are on each other. It's as if we are of one very large body, of which we are; it's the body of Life.

How do miracles happen? The very best I can come up with is there are very major forces at work in and behind the scenes of our everyday lives. They are so very major in fact, as to be subtle; subtle in the fact they seem to blend right into our daily lives with hardly a notice, until maybe a rock comes crashing through your car roof. If you're to be fully aware of these massive powers, it will take training in a sense. You'll need to dump the assumptions you've harbored about things you've always believed to be true. Maybe some things are true and maybe they're not; that part doesn't matter. It's the assuming part that can be the problem.

Just because some man in Rome says miracles only happen to saints doesn't make it true. I believe we're all able to access this power that makes miracles happen. I also believe we're *all* saints in the making. I mean all, because God can't be a part of anything that's not perfection. Each and every one of us has the perfect circumstances and tools for our own perfect spiritual journey.

Think about this: It's impossible to look at one piece of a million-piece jigsaw puzzle and tell what the picture is. Yes, you can pick up some of the pieces and see individually what the piece itself *might* be, but as far as how it pertains to the whole picture, you don't have a clue. In order to put the puzzle together, you have to keep an open mind, take nothing for granted, assume nothing, and do the footwork of putting the pieces into different spots to finally grasp what the Big Picture is.

Our lives are just the same as putting the pieces of a puzzle together. One only has to *re-member*, as in put the members (pieces of our lives) together. In many ways, our minds are finite in the physical sense. It's really hard to grasp spiritual ideas or conceptions and apply logic to them. For me, the only way I've been able to grasp quick glimpses of the Big Picture is by *sensing* them. It just makes *sense* to me when I'm able to comprehend a spiritual idea or conception.

Spiritual happenings are much beyond the logical mind to comprehend if one is still fixed in many of the old ideas or conceptions of the way things are supposed to be. Concerning spiritual matters, there is a spiritual logic one can apply just the same as one would apply logic to material or physical things. Yes, we may get glimpses of the big picture, but those glimpses will come more in the sense of feelings than of pictures in our heads. Some people call it "God Sense" or "God Consciousness."

As of yet, this is why there's such a big split between science and spirituality today. Spirituality can't be proven in the physical sense, or at least the way science wants to prove it. For them to have proof, they have to be able to put their finger on it and say, "Here it is, right here!" Yet, by their own standards, they can't actually prove gravity. They may have a mathematical formula that says it's there, they can work within the boundaries of it or not, but they still can't put their finger on it and say, "This is a piece of gravity, right here." They really don't have a clue as to what gravity is actually made of. All they can come up with is it's some kind of invisible force. Sounds like a part of God to me.

Our whole scientific community needs to quit assuming certain things are certain ways because that's just the way they are. They need to quit saying the only things that are real are the things which can be proven on a piece of paper or a computer screen. I for one have found the real things in my life are the opposite of that. The only things that *are* real are the things I *can't* be put down on a piece of paper. We need to stop this illusion we've created for ourselves; now's the time to wake up.

We have documented proof of tens of thousands of people around the world who've had N.D.E.'s (near death experiences). We also have many documented cases of reincarnation from around the world. Also, what about the people who are truly psychic and can do things that we normal folks can't do? Have you read the books or seen the television shows? Can all these people be wrong? Even if we allowed a few of them to be "a little off of their rocker," there are still many, many more who are legit. I obtain my proof of a psychic's ability through the miraculous healing these people can bring forth with just a conversation with some loved one who's crossed over to the other side.

I believe there are many more mystical happenings which go unreported because of cultural or religious taboos associated with admitting or talking about them. What is science and religion afraid of? Maybe they're afraid that spirituality just might be bigger than they are and they've been misinforming people as to their direction for enlightenment?

It's time for society to call science on this. We need to demand they *prove* He exists, not the other way around. I applaud those few in science who are on the cutting edge of somehow or someway trying to prove there's an Unseen Intelligent Force out there that is much, much bigger than all of us put together. I believe if we dedicated as many resources to finding God (instead of not finding Him), we'd be light years ahead in our enlightenment than we presently are, and I mean that literally. Do you think maybe we wouldn't always be on the edge of World War III if they were to pursue avenues of togetherness versus apartness?

A Journey of Remembering

CHAPTER 16: SEEING THE BIG PICTURE

"To thine self be true." - William Shakespeare

Here's a story for you. When Henry Ford decided to mass-produce the automobile, he needed a source of energy to power his massive auto plant. He hired the finest engineer out of New York to design and build an electrical generating plant. All proceeded as planned and the plant soon came on line; Ford was now in business. As Mr. Ford's plants were manufacturing automobiles one day, the power generating plant shut down for no reason, plunging the plant and assembly line into darkness.

Henry summoned his best maintenance people and put them on the problem. They tested this and tried that, but to no avail. They just couldn't figure out what went wrong or how to fix it. Realizing he was running out of time, Henry sent word to the engineer from New York who originally designed the system and asked him to come to Detroit to see if he could fix the problem. Henry was in a hell of a bind because he was paying all the factory workers to just stand around while orders for his cars backed up; he was losing big money in a hurry. The engineer replied he'd get to Detroit just as fast as he could. The engineer soon arrived and much to Henry's relief, he proceeded to analyze the situation. After only about ten minutes, the generators were up and running with Henry back in business again.

Henry sent notice to thank the engineer for getting there so fast and fixing the problem. He asked the engineer to send him a bill after he arrived back in New York because he didn't have time to mess with it at the moment. About a week after the engineer returned to New York, Henry received a bill in the mail for services rendered. The bill was for $10,000! Henry was in shock, so he sent a letter back asking the engineer to itemize the bill so he could see exactly what he's paying for. A week later an itemized bill came in the mail addressed to Henry Ford, owner of Ford Motor Company. Inside the envelope, Henry found an itemized bill: $128.32 for transportation, $36.78 for miscellaneous expenses, and $9,834.90 for knowing which button to push! Henry had a check drawn up and dispatched to him right away.

Did this really happen? I kind of doubt it, but it's a cute story anyway. I like these kinds of stories because I learn a lot about how things work when I can't seem to understand it any other way. What do I get from this story? First off, I see huge rewards come to those who know how to do something. I apply this especially to spiritual matters. Take the case of miracles for instance. How many great events have just passed me by because I didn't know how to tune into (or push the right button so to speak) seeing (sensing) them? Another thing I get out of this story is how the engineer was able to fix the problem so fast. Ford's maintenance men couldn't fix it because they didn't know how it was *supposed* to work, so they were pretty much just fumbling around in the dark, pardon the pun.

I've been in the HVAC (heating, ventilation, and air conditioning) and electrical field for some time now and I've received many service calls over that time in which I have to go fix a unit that is broken down and not working anymore. Most people could fix their own furnaces or air conditioners if they had knowledge of just one thing, it's called the *sequence of operations*.

Take for instance a high efficiency furnace. There are many more things in the sequence of operations than I'll mention, so I'll just hit the major ones. Number one in the sequence is a call for heat from the thermostat. Next the circuit board confirms it and then continues the sequence, which is checking for any open limits. Then the inducer motor comes on, pressure switches are proved, source of ignition is initiated and proven, gas valve opens, the gas is lit and proven by the flame sensor, and then the blower motor comes on at a pre-set time. The furnace will then run until the desired temperature has been achieved. About ninety percent of the calls I go on, I've diagnosed the problem in five minutes or less. This is not bragging. It just comes from knowing the sequence of operations for furnaces.

A Journey of Remembering

I bring up this illustration for the purpose of applying it to spiritual matters. Once we get knowledge of how spiritual matters work, or their sequence of operations, we'll be able to diagnose problems or difficulties within a short period of time. We'll have a fast track to repairs when they're needed. This is what I've been trying to accomplish throughout this book. I'm putting down in easy to understand terms how spirituality works, or could work for each and every one of us. The parameters are the same for everyone.

We all have great intentions for ourselves. As long as it's only an intention, that's exactly the way it remains, only an intention. Spiritual matters require steady and constant footwork. Do you think the engineer got to be as good as he was overnight? I guarantee you he put in many, many hours of labor to realize his dream. I'm sure he had many setbacks along the way, but they didn't stop him. So it is with us, if our intentions are to have the best life possible, we'll need to exert some effort. Most of the effort will come in the form of learning to think in *different* ways. It won't necessarily be a better or worse way, but it will have to be a different way than what you've been doing if you want to achieve your goals.

Are you happy? Are you having fun? Do you live life joyfully? Is life an adventure for you? Do you look forward to the new day upon waking? Or, is life a struggle just to make ends meet? I think we've all asked ourselves questions like these at one point in time or another. But what were the answers? Is the way you're doing things working for you? Only you can answer that question. You know in your heart-of-hearts (your soul) if it's working for you or not.

All answers come from within, because that's where we get in touch with our soul, and this too is where we find God. If you know God is within, then maybe this saying will have some meaning for you; we've all heard it. It goes like this: "To thine own self be true." (William Shakespeare). There's so much meaning in those six words. Thine self is you, your person and your soul. This statement then, is saying to be true to your soul. Upon reflection of the past, I can personally see in times of so-called trouble, I was not being true to myself (soul). I was not following my soul's prodding; I was taking one hundred years to travel a two-day journey! What I should have done was listen to that little voice inside of me, the same little voice I tried to silence all those years. So if something inside of you is telling you this just seems right, then believe it; be *true* to it.

The next biggest word of importance there is "be." We've touched on this before, but we're going to go over it again. We need things to be repetitious if we're to remember. Remember how I described "being" as not something you get to, or try to get to? You're just there; it's a state or a feeling. You should be able to see what that saying means by what it *doesn't* say. Nowhere in that phrase is the word *try*. Trying is the action of try. Trying gets you nowhere. Being is the place to be. Be truth. Don't talk about it, don't show it, and don't try to achieve it, *be it*. Once you're being truth, you'll be all the things you've dared to imaginine in your wildest dreams.

Why am I talking about beingness while also talking about miracles? It's in this being of truth where you'll *live* miracles. Miracles will become commonplace. You'll experience and feel them all over the place. The uncommon will become the common. The miraculous will be an everyday occurrence, and they *will* happen in everyday occurrences that deal with your car, your home, your occupation, your relationships with your family and friends, or your financial matters; it really doesn't matter what it is. They have to happen in all areas because spirituality (God) is in all areas. Remember my earlier statement, "Either God is (in) everything, or He is (in) nothing?" There will be many times as you grow in your enlightenment that you'll have to stop and ask yourself if you truly believe this statement. Is He really in everything?

Do you believe that once you're well on you way to enlightenment that life is going to just turn all rosy and things will be wonderful? If you answered yes to that, good! You're right, they will be. Life will not be a struggle anymore. Yes, you'll have difficulties of sorts, but they'll not be of the catastrophic type anymore. They'll be of the type for re-membering (as in putting things back together). Remember, you're living a new life now. You're creating it moment by moment.

You've tapped into an unseen force of love, a love that can move mountains. That can be mountains of depression, mountains of

A Journey of Remembering

fear, mountains of resentments and insecurities, and many others like them. Everything will have changed, and yet many things will have not. How can that be? It's in your perception of those things that have changed, and also how you feel about them. Big change will result because of you're seeing the Big Picture and how you fit into it personally.

Spirituality is perfection, it's that simple. How could anything be wrong when there's perfection all around? There can't be, it's impossible. The conditions we have right this very instant are perfect for our soul's enlightenment, and I don't care what those conditions are. It doesn't matter if it's an earthquake in Turkey, a volcano blowing up in Japan, a frozen orange crop in Florida, or a flat tire on the way to a doctor's appointment. The conditions are perfect in their entirety.

Did you notice how after the '99 earthquakes in Turkey, those nations which were bitter enemies of Turkey were united, even if only for a short time? They wanted to help their fellow human beings. The long-standing disagreements over land or philosophies didn't matter. They were being called to a state of compassion and they answered. They offered food, water, clothing, shelter, and logistical help with search dogs and equipment. It takes humbleness to accept help from anyone, let alone someone's enemies. Could such a so-called catastrophe then lead to eventual peace between these nations? So then, was it such a catastrophe?

Yes, lives were lost (40,000 estimated). Many people were hurt and injured, families were broken up, and there was massive property damage. But for those who died, it was their soul's choice to go. Their journey this time around came to an end. In reality, they didn't really die, they just moved on to another dimension. Does it not say in the Bible that God's house has many mansions? (John 14:2) What about the hurt and injured? I will say this: I don't, nor does any human being here on earth, know the soul's journey of another. We're not to judge, lest we be judged. All I know is perfection is present in the souls' course.

I hope I've been helpful to you in looking at the big picture instead of focusing on the little bits of the puzzle. When you look at just the pieces, you'll see imperfections. Yet when all the pieces are put together, you'll remember a perfectly created experience of life and love.

When we're looking at the Big Picture in the world at large, we can also look at the Big Picture when it comes to a flat tire on the car. What if you didn't have a flat tire and kept going, while only two miles down the road you're seriously injured in a car accident? Or, if being late to an appointment, someone stopped by to help you fix the flat tire (they still do this in northern Wisconsin) and you gained a new friend? Who knows *why* you had the flat tire when and where you did; it doesn't matter. You don't have to know the why in order to trust the process of life evolving.

We're looking at just very minuscule pieces of the big picture, so big a picture our finite minds can't comprehend it. There are many things that happen in our lives while looking at it in the short or present term where we won't have a clue as to the "why of it." When looking back with hindsight, we should be able to realize everything that's happened up to this very moment is perfection in action, because it brought us perfectly to this present moment with the present circumstances for our soul's enlightenment.

First, can you *see* the Big Picture now? Second, can you *sense* the Big Picture now? And third, can you *feel* the Big Picture now? Can you feel how it all fits together? You've journeyed far my friend if you can. God bless you!

Chapter 17: Prayer

*Be careful of what you pray for.
You just might get it!*

It was once pointed out to me that prayer is the act of asking and meditation is the act of listening. We'll be discussing meditation in the next chapter but first we're going to take a look at prayer, because we can't expect to receive something we haven't yet desired in the beginning.

We've all prayed even though we might not exactly know why we did it at the time. Some of us prayed just out of sheer necessity because of some calamity that's befalling us; we've reached for that something out there that can save us when nothing else can. Or, maybe we've recited a prayer we were taught as a child just before going to sleep for the night.

How about the Lord's Prayer? This has to be the most popular prayer ever prayed in the history of mankind. I personally never used this prayer much. Prayer for me was usually something I did when I was in big trouble with something or someone. It wasn't really an asking either; it was more like I was begging. My prayer went like this, "God, please get me out of this one and I won't ever do it again, I promise!" The only other times I would pray were when I didn't have something I thought I deserved. I would ask Him to *give* me certain things, like a new car, or more money, or a better marriage, or healthier children, or to help close a certain deal I was working on, which would net me certain fame and fortune.

I can tell you two reasons why those prayers didn't work as efficiently as they could have. The first thing is that prayer is for expressing a desire we *have*. Passing a prayer off as begging is not the most conducive way to accomplish this, because begging is expressing a desire for something we *don't have,* and will remain not having as long as we continue to beg for it. Begging is not a good way to get anything because begging proposes we're not going to personally invest anything to get it. We just want it handed to us on a silver platter. In essence, it's taking a shortcut and with prayer there are no shortcuts.

The second reason for not getting the desired results is I was demanding something of God. By telling Him to give me something, I was requiring God to act in a certain way. It was like saying to God that He has to give me what I want, when I want it, and how I want it. Guess what? God doesn't have to do anything. God has as much free will and choice as we do. And when we *demand* He do or give us something, we've attempted to take away His free will to do it in the time and way He so chooses.

I think that any one of you can tell the difference between a simple request and a demand. How do you want to be treated? Do you like it when someone demands that you do something? I don't know about you, but that never sits well with me. When someone demands we do something a certain way, they've taken away our free will or choice in the matter. That my friends, will lead to rebellion; rebellion to the point of cutting your nose off to spite your own face, or maybe even something worse, like starting a war.

What about *asking* in a prayer? The act of asking is expressing an idea where you feel you're in need or want of something. Remember back in chapter 13 when we discussed what happens when we want or need something; just by the creative force of the words "I want..." or "I need...," we create just that. We create more feelings or experiences of not having a particular thing; more feelings or experiences of need. It's the same with asking. With asking, we're expressing the need or want of something we don't have.

There are a couple of things here I find wanting with this. The first is the statement: Either God is, or He isn't. If He is, then He is everything, or He is nothing. Now, again, do you really believe that statement? If you do, do you really think God would leave you in want or need? If God is everything, what would you need or want that He couldn't provide? What I'm trying to point out here is this: When you are asking, or needing, or wanting, you are in essence saying God *isn't* everything and He can't, or won't provide you with what you desire.

The second thing I find wanting is this "asking" puts God in the light of someone who doesn't feel we should have it all; He wants us to keep wanting, needing, or asking. In essence, He *has* to feel needed. But if He has to feel needed, then how does that fit with the notion of a God not needing anything, because He already has everything? God doesn't need anything from us, but I'm sure He doesn't mind feeling included in our lives. He enjoys being used, but He doesn't have to have it just to make Him who He truly is.

I believe God wants us to experience life in its fullest measure. That's why we came here. I believe we came here with the full understanding that God could and would give us exactly what we desired so we can experience life to its very fullest. He also provides us with fair, just laws and parameters for us to have the life experiences we choose.

I believe we came here with some promises from God; one being that He would never be far from us because He can't get much closer than in the here and now. I also believe we're here with the understanding there will be teachers to help us along the way of enlightenment. These guides may come in many forms. Signs or guideposts can be found in books, people, spiritual guides that take on human form from time-to-time, angels (guardian or otherwise), and animals; it could be *anything*. They would be here all the time, especially in times of strife, disappointment, or losing your way. I can't believe a loving God would allow someone to go on a spiritual journey to somewhere they've never been (at least consciously remembering) without giving them the proper tools, equipment, or maps of some sort so they can *enjoy* (not just survive) the journey and in the end, find their way home.

Don't be afraid to try new things, or seek a new and different path if the one you're on isn't getting you to your desired destination. Yes, you can see great miracles along this path you've chosen, but I believe the majority of miracles will be less than subtle. This reminds me of another story I want to share with you.

This is about a man who was caught in the Mississippi River flood a couple of years back. One of the levies broke and water inundated his farm. There were warnings issued, but the farmer chose to ignore them all. He chose to stay with his farm because he felt such an attachment to it. As he prayed, the water kept rising, and as the water rose he kept seeking higher and higher ground.

As he stood on a small island with the sea of water surrounding him, a rescue boat approached from a distance. As the rescuers fought the rising water to save the man, they were finally able to get near the man and offer assistance. "Get in the boat, we'll save you!" they shouted. "No!" came the reply from the man, "God will save me!" Since they couldn't force the man to get in the boat, the rescuers moved on to search for others.

With the water lapping at his feet, the man observed another boat approaching. Same as before, they shouted for the man to get into the boat. And with the same reply the man said, "No, God will save me!" Off the rescuers went again. Just as the man was about to be overcome by the flood (because he was now standing in water up to his neck) a helicopter approached. They saw the struggling man and sent down a rescue basket for the man to climb into. The man kept shouting something and pushed the basket away while waving them off. The rescue helicopter responded by flying away because they couldn't stay much longer since they were low on fuel.

A short time later the man found himself in the presence of God because he had drowned. Surprisingly, God asked the man, "What in the hell are you doing *here*?" to which the man berated God for not saving his life. "What do you mean?" God asked him. The man replied, "You were supposed to save my life, I believed in you!" At this time God said, "What more was I supposed to do, I sent you two boats and a helicopter!"

Caught you with that ending, huh? I think this is an excellent story of us humans as a whole. We could look a miracle in the mouth and yet push it away because it didn't come in the manner we thought it should, or push it away because we thought we had more time. Maybe we pushed it away because in our minds, we thought God should perform some show stopping miracle and just raise us up and set us on dry ground so we can just go merrily along our way.

I don't believe God performs show-stopping miracles just for the simple reason of impressing us. When your expectations are of seeing lightening bolts, you'll only see sparks. But when you feel you're only going to see sparks, that's when He shows the lightening bolts. Why does it go this way? Because God doesn't have to prove anything to us. Remember, He has free will also. These expectations we have of God is what gets us into trouble. We expect God to act in a certain way and if He doesn't act in that certain way, we figure God can't be God. We've so pigeonholed God, that He can't be a She or maybe even an It. We've pigeonholed God so badly we fail to see Him in all the little things that make up life because that's just what God is - all parts of life including the birds, animals, wind, rain, dirt, water, fish, trees, and all the forces of nature.

Our expectations have gotten us to the point of seeing God only *one* way. Guess what my friends? You're missing the other ninety-nine quadrillion ways He really is. When you have an expectation on anything, you've closed your mind to all the other possibilities there could be. The vast majority of peoples today have closed their minds to the outstanding possibilities of God and His ways.

Exploring this concept a little further, I pretty much believed God didn't have much of a sense of humor about things. He was a cold, calculating type of God and He saw no humor in the things I did or thought. As my prayer life grew to include Him in everything I did, I learned to have fun with prayer, or at least see the humor in it a time or two. I'll relate one of these experiences now.

There's a meditation I experienced which I'm going to relate to you in the next chapter, so I don't want to get too far ahead of myself here. In order to share with you this experience I had with one of my prayers, I need to tell you I always dreamed of building and living in a cabin in the woods. One day while the dream was coming true, I was working on shingling the roof of the cabin. The cabin building process was pretty much a cooperative effort between God and me; it was a real ball, working with God. As the neatly lined up rows of shingles grew higher and higher off the roof edge, I knew I would have to install some roof jacks in order to be able to put the rest of them on because you can only go so far standing on a step ladder.

Before I move on though, I should tell you I'm not any too fond of heights due to the fact that when I was younger (about four

A Journey of Remembering

years old), I fell three stories, and I can say without any doubt in my mind that there's a sudden stop at the bottom! After some reservations, I went up on the roof to install the roof jacks and planks. After that, I hauled up about four bundles of shingles and some nails. On the descent back down the ladder I decided I could use a soda and a cigarette before I began the perilous journey back up the ladder and onto the roof. The roof has a twelve-twelve pitch to it (for every 12" it goes over, it climbs up 12"). This is a pretty steep roof. As I sat there smoking my cigarette, I said a prayer to God to please watch over me so I wouldn't fall.

About this time in my journey, I formed the habit of watching real closely *how* I prayed, because I wanted to make some changes in the way I was doing it. I figured I needed to be a little more specific in my prayers, so this prompted me to add a little something onto the previous prayer. That's when I thought I should add if I *were* to fall, please don't let me get hurt. Proudly I thought to myself, "There, I've got all my bases covered. He's going to watch over me so I don't fall, and just in case I do fall, I've asked Him to watch over me so I don't get hurt." Not a bad prayer, eh? I didn't think so either.

So it's off to the roof I go. I was being pretty confident of God and me on this adventure. "This is going to go good," I said out loud to God. I thought as long as I was going up, I might as well take another bundle of shingles in order to save a trip. Well, I got up all right and proceeded to throw Mr. Hammer into high gear. The more I was up there, the more comfortable I felt about the height. The shingles, God, and I were just cruising right along. Then all of a sudden, time just stood still . . . (I hate it when time stands still because usually something nasty is about to happen for me).

There I was, suspended in mid air. One of the roof jacks let go and this great truth just hit me! The great truth was: *"I'm going down fast and there isn't a damned thing I can do about it!"* I just happened to be turned around when it all began, so at least I was wearing a hole in my ass instead of my face as I was doing 70 mph down the roof. All I could think of at the time was to stay loose when I hit the ground and go with the fall, but don't stiffen up. Before I go any further I need to mention something here and that is I'm a professional faller. I've

A Journey of Remembering

learned if you're going to fall, there's an art to it. It may not look pretty, but it sure saves on the hospital bills.

Anyway, down I go. As I'm approaching the edge of the roof, I'm looking real hard for a good place to land (like I really had a choice). There wasn't too much to choose from though. The cabin is surrounded by some rather large rocks and trees. I made my best guess as to which way I should take off rolling before I hit the ground. Man, I was moving! I hit the ground and kind of acted like a giant spring. I recoiled and rolled to a stop. "Not bad!" I mused to myself as I lay on my back with a half smile on my face. That's when the realization came to me that I wasn't the only thing up there on the roof. There were bundles of shingles, boxes of nails, and planks up there with me. Here it all came down with the same intensity and speed I'd just experienced. I began rolling around trying to dodge the level and planks; I wasn't too worried about the nails. The last piece of equipment to make a mark on me was the uncooperative roof jack.

Wow, what a scene! I lay in a debris field. As I lay there taking an inventory of any broken bones or misplaced parts of my anatomy (miraculously, nothing was where it shouldn't be), I just started laughing out loud. How dumb could I be? I got exactly what I prayed for. If I was going to fall off the roof, then God saved me from getting hurt.

"What's the funny part?" you ask. If I hadn't been so anal retentive in trying to be so specific about my prayers, I would have just left it at: "God, please watch over me while I'm on the roof." But no, I had to show my true faith in God by adding that second part: "Just in case I do fall, save me from being hurt in the process." Remember Nathan, either God is everything or He is nothing? As I lay on the forest floor laughing my ass off, it became crystal clear. How much faith did I have in God that He'd watch over me so I wouldn't fall in the first place? Apparently not enough, because I just *had* to add the second part to the prayer.

You see, there was doubt there after I said the first prayer. I thought to myself, "What if He doesn't watch over me and I fall?" It showed total lack of faith on my part not to leave it with just the first prayer. I don't know, but I happen to see a lot of humor in this little

"Tim Taylor" episode of mine. I could still be a little doubting Thomas at times, but I was getting there. I'll tell you this, it sure taught me a valuable lesson on how to pray, or should I say, *how not* to pray! I honestly believe to this day I wouldn't have fallen if I'd just left it at, "God, please watch over me here, because I'm going somewhere I don't like to go, and that's up!" and then thanked Him for being with me. Can you see the subtle differences here?

You know something? There's nothing like a little pratfall to get God laughing. I could just feel Him just giggling His ass off with me. Notice though, that I didn't say *at* me? He's not that type of God. There's a huge difference between laughing *at* someone and laughing *with* someone. God may have a sense of humor but he doesn't play jokes on us. Thank you God for the humor.

I knew whose fault it was when I fell off of the roof. It was mine, plain and simple. So this time, after a *pack* of cigarettes (I was a bit shaky after that Olympic gold-medal slide off the roof), I went back up on the roof. This time I nailed the roof jack in right. This time I used six nails and was damned sure they were all nailed into a rafter instead of just a sheet of plywood! I'll finish this story with a little saying I've heard. It goes like this, "God looks after drunks and fools, and I'm safe on both counts!"

I can't stress this enough though; it's not so much in *what* we're praying for that seems to be the problem, but in the *how* of it. Humanity has been wanting, asking, begging, pleading, and demanding God save us from ourselves when in reality, we've had the *means* and the *how* to do it all along. Remember the supposed Bible verse which says, "God helps those who help themselves?" (Benjamin Franklin is the true author of this saying). Do you think that has anything to do with the *way* we've been praying? I believe it has everything to do with it. God is available; He has been for a long time now. God is ready, He's been waiting. God's given us directions many times over; it's us who has been having the problem with the execution of those directions.

We seem to be complicating the hell out of something so simple. His laws and parameters are what they are; they can't be broken, even by Him. His laws are simple. He's given us the power to create conditions and circumstances to suit the longings of our own individual souls. Since these powers are so powerful, they must remain within certain boundaries. Here's an example of this: you can't expect to *have* something if all you're doing is still *wanting* it. Again, wanting and having are two different things. One is a state of having and the other is a state of not having and still looking.

Even though wanting and having are two different things, they're the same. They're the same in the fact that they're both *states of beingness*. So, if you're not happy in the state of wanting something different in your life, then change it to the state of having it. You have *all* the power in the universe at your disposal to change it; that's another promise from God. You can either work against the powers that be, or you can work in harmony with them. That is your free choice or free will. It's your call, my friend.

I like to compare it to the laws of gravity. It was once said that humans could never fly, and yet we've sent them to the moon and into orbit around our planet. Once man was able to understand the laws of gravity (you don't have to be able to physically see or touch something to understand it) he was able to work in harmony with the laws, and in the process of understanding and applying them, he was able to accomplish great feats.

Do you think it is such a wonder Jesus could perform the miracles He did by not understanding *how* things worked? He performed the miracles He did because He knew exactly *how* to do it, and *where* the power came from. We have no excuses; we've been shown how and we've been provided with maps for our journey. We have all the necessary tools and equipment. Now, it's time to pick up this kit of spiritual tools and use them. The future, or should I say the present, is in your own hands. You can make it whatever your heart desires, but it has to happen by your own thoughts and beingness. And this brings me right to the final point I'd like to make on prayer.

Remember in the chapter on Beingness where I mentioned the greatest prayer we can ever pray may be a simple statement to God of who we are? This is a simple statement of who we are, not who we want to be, or who we long to be, or who we desire to be, but who we are being right now in this instant. Take the grandest vision of who you would like to be and *be* it. If you've ever dreamed of doing great works in the field of art, then *be* an artist! If your dream is of being wealthy, then *be* a millionaire! If your dream is of writing a book to help others, then write it, *be* an author! Have you ever had a song that you'd like to write someday? Then write it, *be* a songwriter or a singer!

Did I ever dream of writing a book some day? Sure I did, and more. I always had the suspicion that all the things I've been through would one day be helpful to my fellow travelers on their journey of enlightenment. What else would it be useful for? I've found it just isn't any fun if it's not shared with someone else. This is what makes the world go round. That is what joy is. Joy is the soul crying out, saying, "I'm here, I've arrived, I've found my purpose, so let's have fun!" If you're doing something that brings joy to your heart, then you're on your road to enlightenment, whatever that may be. Once you *ex-press* (as in pushing something out) joy, it has to follow the laws and parameters of God just like anything else which is *ex-pressed*. It will come back to you tenfold! You won't be able to give it away fast enough, because in the process, you'll always be getting more than you can ever give away. Understand?

We could all be masters if we'd just claim it and be. It's that simple and instantaneous. I mean that with my whole heart. So in the final analysis, when your prayers are a statement to God of how you're being, then you're a *living* prayer. This may be called the ultimate prayer, nirvana in fact. No longer do you need to be on your knees. *Get off your knees and live! Get off your knees and be!* My last bit of advice here is just what we started this chapter with: Be careful what you pray for, you just might get it.

CHAPTER 18: MEDITATION

Be still and know that I am God. - Psalms 46:10

At times I will sit and think; at other times, I will just sit. This is a lot of the type of meditation I practice. I don't do it nearly enough though. Most meditations involve a process of slowing down, taking a break, and meditating (quieting the mind). Much of meditation is just thinking about something and exploring the options.

I always thought meditation had to be done yoga style, if you know what I mean. You sit on the floor cross-legged, palms up and out in front of you resting on your knees, chanting ooomm, ooomm, over and over again with a little incense burning in the background. I personally have only tried this once and I felt like a pretzel. Holding the form of a pretzel wasn't fun, but I sure enjoyed the aroma of that incense; that's some pretty cool stuff. Anyway, the yoga type of meditation wasn't going to work for me because I have bad knees. I found I needed to explore some different options regarding meditation.

I have read of some fifteen or twenty different ways to meditate. Basically they're pretty much the same as they all have the same desired result. The end result for me is a sense of peace and comfort, a feeling that everything is going to be all right, and a knowing that God cares (a communion of sorts). As I stated in the previous chapter, prayer is for expressing a desire, and meditation is listening for the answer. This statement makes perfect sense to me. It seemed like I was always praying to God in times of trouble or discontent, but I never seemed to slow down long enough for the answers to catch up with me. And that's exactly what meditation is for, the slowing down of the mind and body. It stops the tunnel vision we all get into from time to time; when we become so focused on a problem we can only see it one way.

One of the better forms of meditation I've experienced is the kind where I find a setting where I have some peace and quiet. I sought out this form of meditation because I was in a quandary as to which direction my life should be headed. I would sit and ponder the situation, exploring my options. Next I would take out something spiritual in nature to read. I've found there's no better way out of a fix or a problem than to forget about it (literally, let it go from your mind) and read and ponder something else.

There is another parameter of spirituality I need to discuss here. By totally forgetting about something, we deny it energy to live. Our thoughts are energy; remember they are first in the creation process. So if we quit thinking about something, we deny it energy to live on in our mind and ultimately in our life. It's just like the resentments I wrote about previously. When we focus on something with that much energy, we make it physically appear.

How many times have you worried yourself sick over some bad possible outcome to a situation, only to realize your worst fear came true? That was no coincidence my friend. It had to happen; you brought it to life and nourished it with all the focused energy you gave it. Be careful with this energy, because it's very powerful indeed. What you push against (or obsessively think about) will remain, as long as you give it life energy. Remember this though: This focused energy can be put to good use also. Focus your mind's energy on love for a while and see what happens. I dare you, I double dare you! By focusing energy on furthering your enlightenment, great things can and do happen. We've already talked about some of it in the chapter on miracles and we'll discuss more of it shortly.

Now, getting back to letting go of something you've been dwelling on, this doesn't necessarily have to be done by reading a spiritual book (although I do find this the most consistent way of helping me to let go). You may choose to watch an inspirational T.V. show or movie; it really doesn't matter. Don't you think God can work through any of these if He so desires? Remember, either He is everything or He is nothing. Anyway, find something you feel comfortable with and go for it. Don't have expectations as to what is *supposed* to happen. Going into it with preconceived ideas of how it should be will surely kill the experience. Just go with the flow, let it happen naturally. Let God take you for a ride. He's doing the driving so sit back, relax, and enjoy the view.

After doing whatever it is you need to do to forget about things, just find a comfortable place to sit or lie down and relax. By the way, it wouldn't hurt to say a little prayer now to thank God for this chance to be alone with Him for a while. Close your eyes and focus on an imaginary light right in between your eyes, just above your nose. Sounds a little funky, huh? Don't knock it till you've tried it! Anyway, when the pictures of your mind's eye start coming, let them come. Don't try to make sense of them, just let them be just what they are, because that's exactly what they're supposed to be. Remember, we're along to enjoy the view.

I'm going to share with you my first experience at meditation. I got this really cool meditation cassette tape named *A Wilderness Cabin*. The title of the tape just seemed to fit right in with the dream I had of one day having a cabin in the woods. The meditation tape presented really pretty sounds of birds calling, the wind whispering by, the sound of a waterfall in the distance, and a little background music. (I personally like to listen to rock-n-roll most of the time, but this is a very cool tape, at least when it comes to helping in the meditation process).

Anyway, I rounded up some pillows and a sleeping blanket and laid it out on the floor of my living room (I go all out when I'm into something). I turned off all the lights, but left one on in a distant room. My wife said she would like to join me. So hey what the heck, if you're going to try something new, bring along the family I figured. I inserted the tape into the rack system, cranked it up (which is the way I like music, but isn't necessarily good for meditation). I then dialed it back down to a comfortable level and got relaxed. This woman's voice came on and proceeded to speak real softly on how to breathe while focusing on relaxing the muscles of my body.

I have to break in here and tell the truth, I couldn't focus on anything because I was laughing too hard! The more I tried not to giggle the worse it got. I felt so ridiculous doing this, and in the process of giggling, I'm peeking out of the corner of my eye to see what my wife's up to. Man, she was really getting into this! I start acting funny when I don't feel comfortable doing something for the first time. Needless to say, my wife wasn't into the humor of the moment, so I figured I better shape up and get serious about it.

As the tape is progressing, and I'm mentally relaxing my muscles, you could actually hear the bones along my spine pop back into place; I could actually feel them move. For me, this is a really cool way to start a meditation. Being bent into pretzel form was definitely out from now on. Moving on, the lady on the tape next said I should visualize a cabin set in a green meadow surrounded by forest. There might even be a little pond nearby with ducks and beavers and such. Then she said to just keep playing with this in my mind's eye and just let happen whatever happens. "Cool," I thought. So off I went in my mind. I took a slow walk around the cabin, feeling the cool grass in between my toes and feeling the wind gently caress my face. I stood there for a minute to just enjoy the solitude of the moment. As I stood there, I could hear the birds in the distance. After searching for them for a bit, I finally found them soaring on the gentle breezes.

"What's that?" I asked myself as a whiff of smoke caught me unaware. I turned around to see where it was coming from. I looked to the cabin roof and saw smoke slowly drift up and away from the stone chimney. I approached the front of the cabin and stepped up onto the sturdy porch and entered the doorway into the cabin. Off to my right was a beautiful stone fireplace with a fire softly burning as it sparked and launched out the occasional ember. Off to one side of the fireplace is a wooden rocking chair. I sauntered over to the rocker and comfortably sat down, while relaxing and enjoying the moment. This is one of the most uplifting things for me, just sitting alone by a fire and staring into it; it's very spellbinding. I next glanced over to my left and saw a window in the cabin, perfectly framing the scene of the woods beyond. This was getting to be way too cool! I didn't know what was happening, but I was sure enjoying it.

Just then, as I'm gently rocking back and forth while looking out the window into the meadow, I notice a group of screaming kids stream out of the woods, just having a good old time. As they get closer, a catch a better glimpse of them and can see they are my seven kids. "Son-of-bitch!" I thought to myself. I can't even get away from the kids deep in meditation. This ended my meditation for the evening. Everything went so well up until the point my kids came screaming through. I lay there on the floor feeling disappointed.

As I sat there thinking about what just happened, I thought to myself: "Why the kids though?" I called up my spiritual adviser and asked him what this was all about and why this happened in my meditation? He thought for a moment and then asked me, "What's the most important thing in the world to you right now?" That was a no-brainer. "Besides being sober, my kids," was my reply. Then he said, "So you figure that one of the most important things in your life doesn't belong in your meditation?" (Another preconceived idea on my part.) Well, he got me good on that one. Tears welled up in my eyes as I agreed the kids belonged there and always would.

That was my first journey into the process of meditation. I've since found each meditation as unique and different each time I do it. It's hard not to have expectations (remember about expectations from the last chapter?), but I keep at it. One quick note here though. Through the process of meditation, you're actually *slowing* down your thinking energy. Remember, your thoughts are generating energy at an unbelievable rate, creating everything as we follow the thoughts with words and deeds. The mind is doing warp nine to keep up. When we're able to slow this process down by not thinking about anything, one really cool thing happens. We tap into an energy source that is actually vibrating *faster*! Can't be? I'm telling you it can be, because this is the energy of God you've just tapped into. Slow down so you can go faster. I'll let you think on that one for a while.

I want to share two other meditations I've experienced, one is "coincidental" in nature, and the other one just blew my mind. I'll save the best one for last. Here's an account of the first one which happened early in my sobriety. Things weren't going too well at the time. I really didn't know how to live sober, yet I couldn't go back to the drinking and drugging lifestyle. I owned a cleaning service with many employees, and business wasn't as good as it could have been.

I was on overload as far as employee crap was concerned. I

was tired of being a baby sitter, counselor, and boss. People didn't show up for work, or if they did, they rushed through just to get it done and go home, things were missing on the jobs (theft), and my customers were not happy campers. It seemed like I was getting ten phone calls a day from my clientele complaining and canceling my contracts with them. Also at this time, my personal life was totally in the dumps too, because fifteen years of alcoholism and drug addiction will do that to a person. I wasn't having a good time.

Well, I had enough. I figured this business had to get back to a size I could handle without all the stress involved. I remember standing by my front office door saying the shortened version of the Serenity Prayer because I just lost another cleaning contract and my livelihood was going down the toilet fast. For those of you who aren't familiar with the long version of the prayer, it goes like this: *"God, grant me the serenity to accept the things I cannot change, the courage to change the things I can, and the wisdom to know the difference."*

This was one of those times when I couldn't say the long version of the Serenity Prayer, so I said the shortened version out loud: "God, grant me the serenity to say fuck it!" I also said to God that I didn't care anymore about the business and would He please get it down to a size I could handle. (This was before I learned how not to pray, as in the little trip off the roof). My secretary looked at me like I'd lost my mind. For those of you whom I have just offended by modifying that prayer, I make no apology, for that is what I felt and who I was at the time. That was my surrendering prayer. Because once I say "F*** it!" to something, I've just let go of it because I don't care *what* the outcome is. This is pure letting go. Dejectedly I told my secretary I was going upstairs to my office to be alone. She knew I wasn't in a good way.

Once in my office, I tried to do some reading, but that didn't help. Cranking up the stereo all the way was my next move, but no luck there either. So I just sat there, slumped over my desk with my head in my hands, wondering how in the hell it could have gotten this bad. "God," I said out loud, "it can't get any worse, please help me!" I just sat there moaning. A few seconds later I heard sirens come screaming down the street. I jumped up to look out my second story corner office window. I watched silently as the ambulance came zooming by, light flashing and sirens wailing.

It was like a bolt of lighting hit me. It was as if God was saying, "You think you have it bad? Look my friend, you could have it much worse. That could be you in the ambulance, or maybe someone you dearly love." I thought to myself, "Where did these thoughts come from? They surely aren't mine!" I'm here to tell you God has a way of putting things into perspective. My misery was gone instantly. I walked out of the office, down the stairs, and into my secretary's office. She looked at me in shock. A few minutes prior, she watched me climb the stairs a broken man, but after just a short time I came down healed and with a smile on my face. I knew then everything would be okay.

Just then, the telephone rang; it was another account canceling their contract with me. I think my secretary was a little scared to tell me, thinking I might go off the deep end again, but she mustered up the courage to tell me anyway. I just stood there and laughed. I told her I was getting just what I asked (prayed) for. I asked God to get this down to my right size, and He was doing it! The funny part of it all is God has a different idea of what my right size is, compared to what I thought it should be. I wasn't offended by it though; I just saw it as pretty funny. This was acceptance for me. I thought, "Okay, we'll do it your way, you know best." The really cool part was that I didn't lose another account after that.

Was it just a coincidence that the ambulance went by just when it did? Not in my book. I could see the meaning of it right away when it happened. I knew God had something to do with it, I just didn't know what at the time. I was to find out later on though when He threw a big rock at me on a mountaintop. Humor there, get it? I like to have fun with God. He's got a great sense of humor, not a malicious one.

Looking back on it now, it seems like some of my best meditation experiences occurred when I've really been in the emotional dumps. The answers seem to come very strong and hard during these times. You can't help but know them when they happen. This brings me to the greatest mystical experience I've ever had in meditation.

    This happened to me early in my spiritual quest after sobering up. I was ex-communicated from my church for some time by then, and my family and friends treated me as if I were dead. In their eyes, I didn't exist anymore. I could pass within a couple of feet of my sister walking down the sidewalk and she wouldn't even acknowledge me. Not a wave, not a "Hi," not even a glance or a smile. That was the way I was treated by my whole family. I had five brothers and two sisters plus my parents. Needless to say, I was a little out of the loop.

    One day word reached me through the grapevine, that my next younger brother's wife and two little daughters (whom I never met because of being kicked out of the church) had been killed in a car accident. It was a wintry day with heavy, wet, slushy snow falling. For anyone who's driven in this kind of crap, it's not a fun time. As my sister-in-law was driving down the road, a semi was approaching her and as he went by, his truck threw up a bunch of slushy snow onto the windshield of her car. She couldn't see where she was going and ended up driving head-on into another semi-trailer that was following the first one. My sister-in-law and two very young nieces were killed instantly.

    I was devastated by the news. I didn't know why, but at the time I was as mad at God as I've ever been. I was still young in my journey and figured God was a punishing God. I just couldn't see what these two little girls had done wrong. Christ Almighty, they were barely able to walk and talk. What the hell kind of God was He anyway that could take two young innocent lives like that, not to mention the life of their mother? That night as I was working in a grocery store doing my cleaning, I threw down my dust mop and just started cursing at God out loud. I stood there like some raving maniac, shaking my fists at Him while screaming and sobbing like a madman. "God, why?" was all I could come up with.

    I couldn't understand why this happened and all I could figure out was it was entirely His fault. After all our family had been through over the years, didn't He think enough was enough? When was He going to quit punishing us? For what, I didn't know. I stood at a crossroads with my relationship with Him and I *knew* it. This was the whole kit-and-caboodle rolled into one. Either I was going to get close to Him now, or we would part company and I'd probably never have anything to do with Him ever again. But I just couldn't let the anger and hurt go. I lived in total misery for a couple of days. I think my wife feared for my sanity at the time. At the very least, I know she had a fear that I would go find some comfort in a bottle or drugs. I just couldn't seem to shake it; I couldn't quit thinking about it.

I came home one day in a very disheartened mood and I went to the bedroom to take a nap. I wanted to try and do some reading, as I really needed to figure this situation out. I lay down on the bed and got a book out. I had read part of it before, so I knew it might help me to let go of some things. As I was reading, I came to a part where it told me to relax and meditate on what was written. So I closed my eyes and just relaxed; I didn't fall asleep.

Within seconds of closing my eyes, I was somewhere else. Where I was I didn't know, but it sure scared the hell out of me! I found myself standing somewhere (I can't describe it anymore than that, but it wasn't in a room; there weren't any walls I could see.) The whole place glowed from the inside out. There were maybe thirty or forty people moving around. Some were coming and others were going. There also appeared to be fifteen or twenty people gathered around in a circle and they were surrounding something.

I was scared to death, and I mean total terror! "What the hell did I get myself into now?!" I wondered as panic began to set in. I happened to glance off to my left and noticed a middle aged woman standing there. She smiled at me and I gave her a very weak half-smile back. All of a sudden, her voice came into my head. I heard her, but not through my ears, she was talking *in* my head. She told me I had nothing to fear and I was all right; I was safe. Instantly, my fear was gone. About this time I looked back over to where the fifteen or twenty people were gathering around. As I looked towards them, it was as if my gaze parted them as they slowly stepped back, revealing to me what they were standing around. As I looked across through this tunnel of people, there sat an older gentleman sporting a beard with a look about him which goes beyond description. He seemed to glow from the inside out. Our eyes met and locked onto one another.

A Journey of Remembering

At this very instant I was filled from the inside with **the** most wonderful feeling I've ever felt up to this time or since! I experienced perfect love. I experienced perfect peace. It felt like I was going to burst wide open. It was so overwhelming. It was in this instant when my searching ceased; I found what I've always been searching for. ***I experienced true unconditional love for the first time in my life!*** In just the same way as it started, the experience ended abruptly. I can't tell you how long I was in that meditative state. In one way it seemed like it took an hour or so, but on the other hand, it felt like only a minute or two. I lost all track of time.

I sat up in my bed like a missle ready to launch. "What in the hell was that?" I said softly to myself. I couldn't believe what happened, yet it seemed so real! It was real, I wasn't dreaming. Then it all fell into place; it all made sense. If you care to believe this or not, that's your choice, but I'm telling you the truth, it was real. I ran out of the bedroom looking for my wife. Upon finding her, and from the look on her face, I could tell she was thinking I'd just seen a ghost. She knew something major happened back there in the bedroom, but she didn't know what. She asked me if I was all right. I just blurted out, "I know where the girls went and they're all right!" She looked at me a little bewildered. Sensing this I said, "My nieces, I know where they are, somehow I've been there!" She asked me to tell her about it, which I proceeded to do. We both sat there in tears, because from that moment on, we both *knew* they were okay.

You see, my wife is definitely one of my fellow travelers. She has always been helpful and supportive in my spiritual quest. I don't know how else to describe it, but she is one of my biggest fans. She supported me through it all, good and bad. She's come to expect the unexpected with me. She's the one human who's been the most helpful in opening my mind to the fact that God isn't a nasty God, rather He's a very loving God.

God *knew* I wasn't in a good place at the time of finding out about the car accident; He could feel it. Like I said, it was like one of those times in everybody's life (perhaps the single only time) where it's either do or die. My life was going to be of purpose, or else wasted. I believe God knew it at the time, and He sent something to help me to make up my mind. After the little trip in the bedroom, my fear of dying instantly vanished. No longer did I believe there's a hell where people burn for eternity, or we go off into nothingness. Not only was there no hell or pain, there was perfect love for all. I don't know of any other way to describe it but this: *It's like we're made of love, we're actually made of that feeling!*

Here are some footnotes to this experience. Slowing down and spending some time with God will definitely change your life for the better, it did for me. You see, in the religion I was brought up in, if you're kicked out of the church, you're dead in God's eyes. There's no hope for anyone like me unless I somehow make it back into the church and become reinstated. I had this fear drilled into me for 24 years: If you're out of the loop with the church and God and you die, you go into nothingness for eternity. You're lost to God's memory and become nothing.

Even though I attempted suicide twice in the past, I really didn't feel like dying and being gone for eternity. This was my single greatest fear, the fear of dying. My second greatest fear was someday I would have to answer to God for the things I did wrong, and the punishment wasn't going to be pretty.

This brings me to something else. I believe God killed two birds with one stone with that awe-inspiring meditation. He not only killed my anger and hurt at Him for supposedly taking my nieces for no reason; He also killed my fear of dying. I've been to the other side and lived to tell about it. Personally, I can't wait till it's my time to go, but I will. I have much unfinished business here on earth first.

To this very day, I still don't know the reason for those three souls leaving this earthly plane when they did. It doesn't matter now. I do not, nor could I know, what their life journey was about. I do know that its short duration sure impacted my life for the better! If one of the reasons for their leaving was for me to get to know and experience the God that I understand today, then I'm eternally grateful for their selfless act. I do know one other thing; I *will* be looking them up when I get to the other side, so I can put some more of the pieces of the puzzle together, *to understand and more fully remember.*

I so wish I could transfer those feelings of love and peace I felt and continue to feel to this day. Whenever I think about that meditative revelation even as I write this, the hairs on my arms stand up. Each time I re-live it in its fullness. Now that's the kind of gift that keeps on giving! I wish I had a few of those to pass around at Christmas time or at any other time come to think of it.

Up until now, I've been discussing doing meditation when things aren't going too well. I don't wish for you to get the wrong idea here. Meditation should be done as often as you can. I personally have a little quiet time in the morning as I'm sitting at the kitchen table drinking my milk and having a cigarette. (I know cigarettes aren't good for me. Like I told you, I still have some unfinished business left here on earth).

I also have some quiet time at night after I lie down to go to sleep. It sure beats counting sheep. On Sunday mornings (must have come from my old church days) I go to my place of business and do a lot of reading, writing, and pondering (spiritual stuff). You can throw wondering in there, too. I've been doing a lot of that lately. It's just fun to sit and wonder what's next in the journey and I believe that's the way it's supposed to be. Don't ever lose your childlike wonder; it will serve you well.

To sum up this chapter on meditation, I my best advice is to have fun with it. You'll grow in enlightenment by leaps and bounds if you're listening well. And by listening, I mean a lot. Don't put God in a box; let Him be free to show you His many wonders. If you go to Him with questions, then wait around long enough for the answers. Watch, look, listen, and feel. He can and will come to you through any one of these senses or maybe all of them at the same time. He could be talking to you in the next magazine article you're reading while waiting at the dentist's office, or maybe in the next song you hear on the radio. He may be communicating with you through television shows you watch or a person you walk into at the restaurant. He may speak to you with an eagle flying by, or maybe in a child's song you hear. If you limit God, you limit yourself and your experience of Him. Remember anything is possible in God's plan.

I just mentioned God might come to you in the next eagle you see. I'll now explain what I mean by that. I rarely used to see eagles before and it's not because there weren't many at the time. I believe it was because I didn't know what they meant. Eagles are one of God's messengers. Do you know what an eagle does when there's a bad storm approaching? All other birds will seek refuge from the storm either by finding a place to hide and sit it out until it's over, or they'll fly away putting some distance between them and the storm. An eagle, on the other hand does neither of these things; it doesn't have to. It simply flies above the storm. Think about the message they are relating here. Can you see why eagles are such messengers of God?

How many times have you seen personal or spiritual storms gathering on the horizon and you hid while weathering it out until they were done? How many times have you taken off running, thinking you just needed to place a little distance between you and the storm, but eventually it caught up to you anyway? Stop, quit running. Imitate the eagle and rise *above* the storm. You don't need to run from it nor hide from it, just rise above it. I now see eagles as good omens because they always remind me God is nearby (something I can see with my physical eyes) and I don't have to run from anything anymore. Just let it *be*. Guess what? The Native Americans had it right the whole time! One word of caution though, you probably won't see eagles if you're out *looking* for them. I know this sounds a little crazy, but don't look for them, they'll find you.

I have this friend of mine (Dennis is his name) and we were discussing what eagles meant and what messages they give a person. He went right out and started looking for eagles after that. When we talked a few weeks later and he mentioned how he'd been looking for eagles and couldn't find any, that's when I suggested to him to quit *looking* for them, because they'll find you when the time is right. God bless him because he was actually able to quit looking for them, and now he sees eagles all the time. It wasn't long after our discussion he mentioned to me when he returned home from work one day, he had two of them flying real low over his house. I thought that was pretty cool. So go, *not* looking for eagles and other signs or messages, just *be,* and the messages will find you, my friend.

The last thing I'd like to discuss with you in this chapter is the letting go of something. It's only by letting go of something that you truly know what you had in the first place. How can that be? First off, the only way to let go of something is to first pick it up. Simple enough, right? You have to first pick up a ball with your hand before you can give it to someone else, correct? So, when you physically picked the ball up, you had the feeling of *controlling* it. You could either give it to someone else, or put it back down. But through the *act of giving* it to someone, you *experienced* the feeling of *once having had it*, so it's through the experience of giving it away that you have the proof of once having had it. I know this sounds a little confusing and it actually is.

It's hard to describe some spiritual things in a physical sense. Let me use the state of being called compassion as an example. You can feel compassion, but you have to give it away to truly experience it. It's the same with the ball. When you give it to someone else you experience the feeling of *having had it*. It's only by that experience that you'll *know* you have compassion by the very act of being it. How could you be compassionate to someone if you didn't have it to give away? Can you see the complexity of it? I guess when you look at it backwards, it might make more sense. To truly know what you have, you have to give it away; you have to let it go.

God designed the system perfectly by always making sure we have plenty to give away. He knows we can't keep giving something away if we don't have it in the first place. This takes us back around again to either God is everything (or gives everything), or He is nothing (or has nothing to give). God has designed the system to always come back around on itself; this is perfect efficiency, nothing is lost. All energy comes back around into itself. Now you know why the Native Americans use the symbol of the circle so much, because all of life's journeys are but a big circular path through God, not around Him. And I mean, through God, for we're all a part *of* Him, not a part *from* Him.

So it is with my friend Dennis looking for eagles. He had to let go of the act of *looking* for eagles before he could truly *see* the eagles. It was only by not possessing or trying to control the experience that he could see and experience it fully. Now you should be able to see why relationships don't and can't work when one is trying to control the other. This is going against two laws of God. The first law is love is unconditional, it can't possess. The second law it breaks is that you can't control the other person, for the very act of trying to control them will kill the relationship instantly. We have to let go to truly know and experience what unconditional love is. Once we've done that, then we'll experience love because love is letting go and not possessing. Loving someone unconditionally means they have total, unfettered freedom to just be; *no* strings attached.

So in the final analysis, this is the way it works. To truly have something, you must first express it or give it away. The tighter you hold onto something, the faster you'll kill it. You've all heard about the little boy who found a baby bird? He picked the baby bird up and ran to show his mother what he found, but as he opened his hands to show her, the baby bird lay there motionless; it was dead. He hung onto the bird so tightly so as to not let it get away that he killed it. That is the meaning behind "Let go and let God."

There is also the saying that if you truly want to know if something is yours, then let it go. If it comes back to you then it was yours to let go, but if it doesn't come back, then you never had it in the first place. I've experienced this a time or two in my life. I am going to relate to you one of my personal experiences of having to let go of something I very dearly loved, and still do. This "something" I love is two of my children, Autumn and Benny.

While in my first marriage, I went looking for something I felt was missing at home. I felt more unneeded and unloved as each new child came along. As each of the four was born, I felt like I was getting pushed further and further out of the picture. I had other issues going on in my life at the time that wasn't helping the situation either. As time went by, I soon found myself in a relationship with someone other than my wife. I'm not going into greater detail here because it serves no purpose. I needed to tell you about how it happened so you'll be better able to understand why I did what I did.

As with some relationships, after they've been going on for a while, things happen. It happened twice in this relationship because I had two children with this woman. This was the very reason for my split with the church, family, and friends. When the church became aware of my doings, they proceeded to tell me to pay the child support, but I wasn't to have *any* contact with the children because it would be too confusing to them. While in a meeting with the church elders, they told me this was the way I would have to do things if I wanted to remain in the church. If I chose to keep seeing the children, then I would have to suffer the punishment of the church which meant total banishment.

    I couldn't believe my ears! I had to agree with them that the way these two children came into the world wasn't too kosher as viewed by church and society standards. It didn't make any sense to me to fix a wrong with another wrong. I felt it was totally wrong to deny these children; it wasn't their fault as to what I personally let happen in my life. I knew what would happen if I didn't do things the way the church wanted me to, but I couldn't help my self. It would mean total and permanent ex-communication from all my friends and family. This was the price I would have to pay, and I was willing to pay it. After them telling me how I was to act in this situation, I told them how they should act!

    I not so politely told them *where* they could stick that Bible of theirs and out I walked, never to return! This may sound strange, but I felt a real sense of freedom after I left there. No more was I going to let some institution run my life. It kind of felt like the time I stood up to salute the flag in grade school. Getting back to letting go of something, I did pay my child support, and I did have a wonderful relationship with my two children, at least for a while. The same thing couldn't be said of the relationship with their mother. As time progressed, drugs and drinking (and everything that goes with it) laid claim to my sanity and my life. My relationship with the children's mom soured quickly and ended.

    I still had some visitation rights, which I used as often as I could, or as often as she would allow. But as time went by, things became more and more difficult between their mother and me. She met someone else and married him, which was just fine by me, but she started going nuts on the kids. She changed their last names, which didn't sit right with me (legally there was nothing I could do about it). She told them my other children were bad kids (which they weren't) and also denied me my visitation times with the kids. When I was able to get them for a weekend or so I would try to make the best of it, but that was extremely tough.

When they came over, they'd tell me all the things they did with their new dad. I would tell them over and over again he wasn't their dad, I was! But the more I did that, the worse it made things between Benny, Autumn, and me. After about six months of this, I could feel them slipping away. This time I redoubled my efforts and got the courts involved. I wanted fixed visitation rights with my children, and I wanted the law to make sure I got them. So I started legal proceedings in the matter.

I petitioned the court to set something up regarding my visitation rights. They scheduled an appointment for their mother and me to meet with a mediator to try and work things out in the hope this wouldn't have to be dragged through the courts. So Vickie and I went to the mediation session. I went there looking for a minimum of every other weekend and some holidays with the kids. Their mother wasn't going to hear of this; she threw a fit for almost two and a half hours protesting how bad a father I was.

Not once would she look at the role she had played in this relationship (this all happened about a year after my sobering up). After two and a half hours of taking her bullshit, I blew a cork! I let her have it with both barrels; I had taken it long enough. Screw the mister nice guy of being understanding and kind. All she wanted to do was point out all my character failings and not look at her own. She knew where my buttons were, and I let her hit every one. After seeing the way it was going because she wouldn't compromise an inch, I said, "Enough, I'm done fighting over this, this isn't getting us anywhere."

After it was all said and done, I agreed to visitation rights of one day per month for less than 24 hours! Christ, that was less than I had before I went in! I couldn't believe it, I never abused those kids; I only loved them. Here I was putting my life back together, and I just wanted to show the kids I could be a better dad than I was before. It sucked and I knew it, but I agreed to try it for six months and see how it went. What a joke, I agreed to be a dad to them for what amounted to twelve days out of a year. How the hell can anyone be a dad for only twelve days out of a year?

Over the next few months I could see this arrangement wasn't working, and it was doing extreme damage to the kids. As the last of the six-month visitation arrived, I knew it was the end. I won't deny what I did next was just as much for my own sanity as it was for theirs. The last time they were over was for Christmas, which she didn't let happen until January some time. I picked them up, brought them home, and they went right for the tree to get their Christmas presents. They opened their presents, which probably took twenty minutes, and then put their coats on and were ready to go home! As Autumn walked into the kitchen, our eyes met and locked. I could see the "sparkle" was gone. I knew the time had come to let them go.

After Autumn left the room, I looked at Vickie and said, "The light's gone out in Autumn's eyes. Her spirit is being crushed by her mom and me fighting all the time. Someone has to let go, I can't bear this anymore." I told Vickie I was going to take them home. On the way there, I stopped at my office and told them what I was going to do. I explained that the fighting was all over and it wasn't their fault, but I wasn't going to be seeing them anymore. I was going to give up my parental rights so their new dad could adopt them. How do you explain to kids aged nine and eleven that what you're doing is because you love them so much?

Needless to say, this was a very dark night for me, one of my darkest ever. After all I had been through, giving up my family and friends in order to right a wrong as best I could, and then letting it all go, just didn't seem fair. But the needs of my children had to come first. I couldn't honestly say I loved them and yet continue to put them through hell. So that's the way it ended, on May 20, 1996. I went to court to let them go. You may not agree with what I did, that's okay, but I *knew* then, as I do now, it was the best thing I could have done for Benny and Autumn. I've left it all in God's care since that day.

I know we seemed to have really gotten off the track here a bit since we're dealing with meditation, but it fits in here so nicely. We need to let go of ideas, conceptions, notions, or ways of doing things that haven't been working. The ways that haven't been working may be doing just as much damage to others as to us. Getting back to meditation, meditation is a journey in and of itself. You won't go far with preconceived ideas on *how* it should be, or *how* it should happen. God wants us to enjoy ourselves, so let go and experience God in His rich vastness and greatness. This leads us to the following chapters. You'll get to experience God in all things, big and small.

A Journey of Remembering

CHAPTER 19: GOD IS IN THE ALL OF IT.

*God only blesses those that can receive it.
And that's everyone!*

That statement is very true. We've all heard of blessings in disguise, right? What's a blessing in disguise? Just what it says, it's a blessing that may be concealed inside of something else. It could be a misfortune, or a hindrance of some kind, even a major emotional hurdle. It could even be disguised in another blessing. Either way, a blessing is still a blessing, and they come in many forms.

How many times have you looked back at your life and seen what seemed to be a real difficult situation at the time, only to find out down the road it was the best thing that could've happened to you. What changed? Your perspective of it changed. With hindsight you see how it fits into the whole scheme of things, as it applies to your journey. You can look at it from the outside now, instead of being in the middle of it.

If you're on the road of enlightenment, you should be able to see now many of the hardships you experienced as blessings from God, and if you don't see all of them as being blessings, then wait, you will. Be careful when judging what is presently happening right now, because it could be the best thing that's ever happened to you, if you let it. I want to share with you the story of the cabin I experienced in meditation and how it came to be.

I'm sharing this in hopes you'll be able to see the blessings, but if you choose to see them as coincidences that's all right too. Either way, I hope this will drive home the point of how spirituality happens in everyday occurrences if you choose to see them. Just be aware of the subtle things that begin to happen in your life.

A Journey of Remembering

Keep a close watch out for all those little coincidences, accidents, or signs that seem to be pointing or prodding you in the direction you'll need to go as respects to fulfilling your dreams. Notice things as they begin falling into place all on their own without any help from you. You will need to keep one thing in mind though. You must remain open to *all* possibilities, because if you're only focused on a certain outcome, then there will surely be disappointments along the way. You'll be disappointed when things don't work out exactly as you figured on in the beginning, so just stay loose and go with the flow of creation.

This is a "we" story because I'd be lying to say I did it all by myself. God helped me tremendously, as well as my wife. I also had help from my son Travis, my nephew Timmy and his girlfriend, as well as a few other friends and acquaintances. They were all part of the plan.

My wife and I wanted to build a cabin which would be set deep in the woods and would have a rustic feel to it, because that's what we both loved. We wanted something that would be both simple and homey. We also wanted to do it inexpensively as we didn't want to borrow money, but we first needed to find a piece of land on which to build the cabin.

We kept alert as we were out driving around the countryside, keeping an eye peeled for those occasional realtor signs. We'd find something and inquire about it only to find out it just wouldn't work. Either the asking price was too high or the land sat smack dab in the middle of a swamp! I suppose we looked for a month or two, and didn't find anything to fit the bill. I was getting a little depressed because it wasn't happening the way I thought it should.

This is when Vickie pointed out to me that maybe I should try to take it easy (she knows once I get going on something, there's no stopping me). She pointed out it may not be happening yet because God is still looking for the right place. That made me stop and see *I* had been trying to *make* things happen, instead of just *letting* them happen on their own. You know God, He's like real estate; the three most important things about Him are location, location, location!

Anyway, that put things into perspective for me. I just needed to sit back and relax a bit, quit trying to force it, and let God take care of it. I'm sure He could find something which would be out of this world. After I quit focusing on finding a piece of land on which to build, I was reading a shoppers guide one night looking for a deal on something else, when I noticed an ad for five acres of land in the Blue Hills (the Blue Hills are located in northern Wisconsin, about twenty miles from where we presently lived).

I wanted more land because I like lots of elbowroom, but the price was right as the seller was only asking $6,000 for the five acres. So I thought I'd call and find out about it. He said the lot was near the end of a half-mile private road, and the southern lot line bordered thousands of acres of county land. Hell, this sounded pretty good! I would get lots of room around me, and I wouldn't have to pay the property taxes on it. It also sounded good due to the fact that the price wasn't bad for the five acres. Land here in northern Wisconsin was going for much more than that at the time.

So my wife and I went for a road trip to check it out. We found it pretty easily and proceeded to walk around the land. I would like to say it took all of five minutes to agree God had found the perfect spot for the cabin, but in reality, we both decided this was exactly what we were looking for even before we saw the actual lot. We scrounged up some money and bought it immediately!

The land sits on top of one of the higher peaks in the area. It has beautiful hardwood trees on it, and a gentle slope to the south. Down below the hill a bit is Murphy Flowage, a beautiful small lake and dam where Vickie used to come when she was younger to swim and bask in the hot summer sun. In her younger days she always told her friends that one day she'd live up here in the Hills by Murphy Flowage (I didn't find this out until *after* we bought the land).

During the time we were looking for land, I told Vickie I didn't want to live near Birchwood, which is the closest town to the land. I didn't know why, but that was the last place I wanted to build a cabin (I had a slightly closed mind). After seeing the land, I literally forgot about the fact I didn't want to live in the area. So to put this all together, it was just too much of a quirk of fate the land happened to be where Vickie told everyone this was where she was going to live one day. God found us one of the last available pieces of land close to the flowage. What a blessing, huh? Can you see the start of something here? We (mainly me) had let go, and little miracles started happening, and would continue to happen right up to the present.

Now we had the land, but what were we going to build the cabin out of? I've never really liked the idea of throwing away perfectly good stuff, so I sat down to think of some of the building materials I already had that we could use, instead of going out and buying everything brand new. We had plenty of things to put *inside* the cabin because I collected antiques for years, but we had nothing to build it out of. So we stayed open to the possibilities. I talked with many of my friends to see if they had any cool ideas that we could borrow. One suggested we explore the possibility of building it out of stone (the Blue Hills is known for its rocks; they're everywhere) but this was too much work in that venture. I didn't want to have to finish it while sitting in a wheelchair with a broken back from lifting all the rocks. We thought about a log cabin, but it was too expensive, plus some prime lumber would have to be destroyed to get it. So that idea was out.

We were running out of options, when one day as I was going on a service call way out in the boonies, I drove past this farm that had a big "For Sale" sign on the old barn. "Hey, what about using that old barn for materials?" I thought to myself. That could be a cheap source of recyclable lumber, and it would give us the rustic look we wanted. I was quite sure it had many old beams and timbers in it. How much the owner wanted for the barn seemed to be a stumbling block though. We were on a budget and the budget didn't include much, that's for sure.

I told Vickie about the barn when I got home from work that day. Off on another road trip we went so she could see it. She really liked the idea, but knew it would include a lot of very hard work because the barn was still standing, and it would have to come down and be dismantled. The lumber would have to be gone through and sorted, with the nails being removed beforehand. Then it would all have to be hauled away to be put into storage until the following spring, as it was getting too late in the year to start building the cabin. When she saw the barn, she fell in love with it, and said, "Let's go for

A Journey of Remembering

it!" Neither one of us had ever torn a barn down before, though I helped put one up when I was in high school. Vickie is pretty much game for any new experience. She always figures that the harm comes in *not* trying something new.

So the next time I went past the old farm, I stopped to see how much the gentleman wanted for it. He just happened to be home at the time (another blessing). Another coincidence was that I had another service call in this same area within a couple of days of looking at the barn. Ordinarily, I hardly get five calls to that area in a whole year! See how efficient God can be? He actually made it happen that I could make a little money on the service call while being in the right place at the right time in order to be able to catch this gentleman at home.

I knocked on the front door and an older woman opened it. I told her I stopped to inquire about the barn they had for sale. She said she'd have to go get her husband because that was his deal. A minute or two later an elderly man appeared, and I asked him how much he was asking for the barn. He said, "I'm looking for someone to take it down." I told him I understood that, but how much money did he want for someone to take it down and get it out of there? "I just want someone to take it down!" he replied rather sternly. I was in total confusion now. He had a "For Sale" sign on it, yet he kept insisting he just wanted someone to take it down. Finally I was able to get it straightened out and understood that he didn't want any money - even though there was a "For Sale" sign on it - he just wanted it down and gone.

Well, I'll tell you what, I couldn't sign the papers fast enough! That's a God sent deal if you ask me. Never in my wildest dreams did I figure we'd get it for free. Initially, I almost didn't stop to inquire about the barn because of the "For Sale" sign on it, but a little voice inside my head said to at least stop and see how much he wanted for the barn. What's the worst thing that could happen? It doesn't cost anything to ask. Oh, I knew it was going to cost me some gas money and a few tools, and maybe a few trips to the chiropractor, but I *know* a deal when I see one. I couldn't get home fast enough to tell Vickie what happened. Our dreams were becoming a reality. What a rush!

We now had the lumber, and what beautiful lumber it was.

Huge old beams, some nearly twenty feet long, eight inches square, and straight as an arrow. The beams were put together with wooden dowels. This "old girl" was a classic. I figured the barn was built by hand around the turn of the twentieth century and it was in perfect shape to boot! Then the work part of the dream began. As with all dreams, it required much fortitude and sweat. It wouldn't mean as much if a dream is just handed to you, I'll promise you that. Yes, I stand by my previous statement that things will just fall into place without much effort on your part, but that doesn't mean you won't have to put *something* into it. That something is your "being."

So off to work we went. We began the process by tearing off an old calf shed on the one side of it; that didn't go too badly. It was kind of dirty work, but it went well. Then we proceeded to tear off the siding of the barn itself, as this would allow us to take some of the structural rigidity out of it when it came time to pull it down. The roof was next, and there was no way in hell I was going up there to tear that off! That thing had to come down to me. So I talked to a couple of friends of mine, one being my spiritual advisor who just happened to work for a mutual friend of ours who owned two wreckers for hauling cars. We figured if we loosened up the main structural supports of the barn, we'd be able to pull it over sideways and then it would fall down on its own; that is, if we could get a high enough pull on it. Ed's always looking for a challenge too, so he fit right in.

We set up the big day for the dropping of the barn on the following weekend as we all had time off of work. We had to figure in the car traffic as well, because the barn sat about thirty-five feet from the main road. This was going to be tricky because of the barn's location. There was also a utility pole standing about six feet from the barn. Within five feet of the backside of the barn, was a brand new eighty-foot pole shed, and on the other side was a big drop off down to the river which ran by. I'll tell you what, for that barn to come down *right*, it would have to land in a perfect position so it wouldn't take out something expensive to replace, like a new pole shed or a utility pole.

The big day arrived and we had cameras in hand for the big event. I also brought along a chain saw for some last minute remodeling, if you know what I mean. Ed and Tommy arrived with the wreckers. Ed came over to me to let me know what happened along the way over to the barn. He knew of the importance of eagles too and told me that on his way over, he'd been praying to God to let everything be okay and asked that no one would get hurt. Just as he finished his prayer driving the wrecker down the road, from out of nowhere an eagle came alongside him and flew about fifteen feet off of the ground. It flew along side for a ways, then flew ahead and landed in the ditch. It just sat there and watched him drive by!

Needless to say, I was impressed! I was praying all the way there for God to watch over us and see to it that everything would be okay. I pictured in my mind that eagle flying by Ed in the wrecker, and I knew then everything would be okay. Somehow those eagles just seem to keep appearing out of nowhere to drop a little message off on their way.

Next, we proceeded to put steel cables into place (which just happened to be there in the barn, something else that I didn't have to buy) and hooked the wreckers up to them. Then I went into the barn loft to start cutting most of the way through the main supports and beams. This was a tense time for me because I didn't know if the whole thing might come crashing down on top of me (little did I know how much this old girl had left it her). But I said another quick prayer and got done with the job of cutting through the supports. Finally, we were all ready to start pulling. I stayed on the road to watch from the end to see how it was coming. Ed and Tom cranked up the winches and started pulling. The old barn began to creak and groan as it moved ever so slowly to the side, looking good though.

The front ends of the wreckers literally came right off the ground about a foot or so, and then we'd quit pulling for a bit. We'd let the barn catch up to the pull so to speak, and when the wreckers would slowly settle back down to the ground we'd start pulling again. All of a sudden one of the steel cables let go! That barn roof was a good foot over center when it happened. The barn shot back towards the new pole shed and I got a lump in my throat. Everyone held their breath. The barn wobbled back and forth a couple of times and settled still. We all took a deep breath at the same time. Wow, that was a close call! Thank you God was all that went through my mind at the time.

A Journey of Remembering

I found where the cable let go and I proceeded to repair it. We were ready to pull again in about fifteen minutes. Into high gear the wreckers went again. Pull and wait. Pull and wait. Again it happened! The other cable let go, this time. Again we all held our breaths. The old girl wiggled and wobbled but she didn't fall down. I was beginning to question the sanity of what we were doing. Maybe this wasn't such a great idea after all. Oh well, third time's a charm, so we decided to pull on her one more time.

Same as before, I fixed the cable clamps and we started pulling. If nothing else, that old barn sure should have been loosened up by now with all the pulling and wiggling. Again it was pull and wait, pull and wait. The cables seemed to be holding this time, so I gave the okay wave to keep pulling. Just a little bit more I figured. To be honest, as far over center as the roof was sitting, I figured it would've come down by now. But this old girl sat there and weathered many a howling storms for over a hundred years and she wasn't going to come down easily. I gained a new respect for the men who built this thing in the beginning. They really knew how to put something up which lasted *more* than a lifetime!

We pulled a little more. More creaking and groaning and this time I could hear some major snapping and popping going on. The roof peak was almost three foot over center when it just seemed to hang there in the air. "Pull fast and hard," I screamed. "Keep pulling, we've got her, and she's coming down this time!" Then the forces of gravity took over and down she came with one big crash! We all stood there in stunned silence for a bit as we watched the dust settle down ever so slowly. The old girl put up quite a fight and I know we all had a lot of respect for her. Then the cheers and hollering started. We'd done it! The barn landed perfectly, and I mean perfectly! It was like God had grabbed it with His hand and just set it in the perfect spot. Now I could tear off the roof; it was down to my level.

I looked at Ed and he smiled that smile of his, which says so much. The eagle was right again; it worked out perfectly. We still had some film left in the camera, so we finished it off with pictures of the "barn tearing down crew." What a day! And that's the way the day ended as we got one step closer to realizing our dream of having a cabin in the woods.

It took a little over two months of working on weekends, evenings, and any other spare time we could find, to finally complete the job of dismantling and hauling the old barn away. Vickie and I had grown to appreciate our freedom and independence of each other, but working this much together was going to be interesting. Would I be able to allow her to do things the way she needed to do them, or was I going to insist that everything be done my way? I grudgingly let her do things the way she wanted to, just for the simple fact that my way of doing things doesn't necessarily make it the *only* way, unless I thought she could possibly get hurt by the way she was going about something. After that, I just let her *be* because that's the most loving thing I could do, both for her and myself. I learned a lot about myself through this time and so did Vickie. I don't think I'd be stretching it to say we both grew a lot in the time we spent together.

It was a lot of fun in many ways, in spite of having to pull tens of thousands of nails out of the old barn boards, and picking up a sliver or two. I can remember this one day. It was cold and overcast, snowflakes were hitting us in the ass, and we were both sitting there pulling out nails and dreaming of how the cabin would look when it was completed. We'd throw different ideas at each other, mull them over for a bit, and then throw something else back at the other one. It taught me a lot about compromise and just letting go in order to allow Vickie to have her dreams also.

Once you put a dream into motion, it's really uncanny how things just seem to start falling into place. We needed windows and doors for the cabin. As I was working on a customer's home which was being remodeled, I noticed they were putting all new windows and doors in. Curiously I asked them what they were going to do with the windows they pulled out, as they were sitting near the demolition dumpster. They said they were getting thrown away and I could have them if I wanted. Cool, I grabbed them right up.

Then the owners remarked the bathroom was also going to be totally redone, so I asked them what they were going to do with the cast iron bathtub with the claw feet, because I could use that in the cabin. I offered to buy it from them, but they refused and mentioned that if it wasn't out of the house in fifteen minutes, they were taking a sledgehammer to it! So I yelled at Dan (he works with me) "Grab the other end of this tub and let's get the hell out of here!" I don't need to be hit over the head with a 2 x 4 anymore to get me moving on deals like that.

Over the months of building the cabin I would run into more and more deals like that; a little something here, a little something there. It all just kept falling into place, little by little. Each time it happened, I'd know immediately who was behind it all. Once you've gotten to the point of making your dream a reality, then I believe unseen forces are put into motion to get you just what's needed to see the dream through to its fulfillment.

Some of the building materials in the cabin are new, but I would guess seventy-five percent of the materials are recycled from other homes and places. Now, don't get me wrong, Vickie and I both like new and fine things, but we don't *have to* have them, if you know what I mean. Sometimes in the pursuit of a dream, you may have to scale things back a bit, which can be a real blessing in disguise. The cabin turned out to be something beyond our wildest dreams.

Today, I stand in awe when I sit and think about how everything just came together for the dream to be realized. It was like there was perfection at work there, because when God is involved, it can't go any way but perfectly. Remember, either He is everything or He is nothing. Looking back on it as I was writing this down for you, I can see the times I struggled were when I was trying to push things, and make them happen. I learned a lot by just letting go and letting God take care of the details.

That's the part I was talking about when I said in realizing a dream, you may have to stand back a bit and just let it happen naturally on its own timetable. Just put the dream into motion, and God will take care of the rest. I don't mean to say this just applies to dreams; it could include anything in your present life. Whenever you meet resistance in anything now, it's a signal to back off, because you're trying to do God's job. Life is not supposed to be a chore or drudgery. I believe it's meant to be something that's to be enjoyed, something to have fun with, and so it will be.

A Journey of Remembering

CHAPTER 20: QUIT WORRYING, START WONDERING!

"Numberless are the world's wonders, but none more wonderful than man."
Sophocles

You want to have a little fun with something? Do this: Quit worrying about things and start *wondering* about them. Wonder how things can be changed around so you may know and experience success in your life. If you do this, you'll be doing four things differently. The first one is by stopping the worrying over things you quit trying to control the outcome of the situation. Remember, it's by surrendering that one gets?

The second thing you'll be doing differently is that you'll now be focusing on how God can fix the situation, not on how you have to. You'll be putting the powers of creation we all have at our disposal into a positive mode. Positive in the sense it will help you on your journey of enlightenment, not hinder it.

And the third thing you'll be doing differently (which I believe is the most important), is when you're worrying about something, you're focusing on the problem, not the solution. It's that simple! When you're focusing on a problem, you're putting focus on the negative aspects of the situation, but when you're wondering, you're putting your focus of energy on the solution; a positive aspect. Can you see the difference? It's a big one. How much of your life have you been focusing on the negative aspects of the problems when all along you should have been focusing on the solution. I have a suspicion some of you have done it as much as I have in the past.

A Journey of Remembering

The fourth thing to be different is in the way you use your mental creative energy. Worrying is not fun; worrying is very draining. Ever notice how during and after you've worried over something, how very drained you feel both mentally and physically? Worrying is *very* detrimental to the human body. This is called stress, and stress will either mutate or kill the very cells of your physical body.

Now, when you're wondering about something, doesn't it seem to be an uplifting sort of experience or feeling? I can prove this to you real quick. Take a few minutes please and put this book down and find something to worry about. I'm not kidding, try it. It'll be worth your time to indulge me on this to prove to yourself how much time and energy you can save in the long run, not to mention the stress it'll cut out of your life.

After you've worked yourself into a lather worrying about something, take a deep breath and relax; let go of the worry and *quit* the action of worrying about it. As you're relaxing and letting go, I want you to embrace something different now. It's simple, but not always so easy do. Quit the action of worrying about the problem now and *wonder* about the solution. Just sit there and *wonder* how this thing is going to be fixed, and not necessarily by any action of your own. Let your mind go with it, and explore all the possibilities there could ever be. Feels a lot better than worrying, no? Now that you've done this, apply it to all your worries and a great thing will happen.

By changing a worry into a wonder, you won't have any more worries. I know this sounds simple, but it's true. And I've saved the best for last; expect miracles! Expect to see them, expect to feel them, and expect to experience them. As I outlined back in Chapter 15, a miracle is: a *wonder*ful thing; or an act or happening attributed to a *supernatural power*; or a *wonder*. Do you see why the action of wondering, or its corresponding state of being, is so much better for your soul, mind, and body, versus the action or state of worrying? We all have the power and means to create miracles all the time. I call this process *"miracling."* All you have to do is when you find yourself worrying over something is to stop worrying about it, and start *wondering* how the situation is going to be fixed. Mentally putting yourself into the state of *wonder* (or miracling) puts the whole process

A Journey of Remembering

into motion. I believe we play a much larger role in making miracles happen than we give ourselves credit for.

I have a story for you to ponder which fits right in with what we've been discussing here. It's about a few hamburger stand owners in this small town which sit next to each other on the same street. Each owner thinks they have the best tasting hamburger in town. One of the owners was sitting and worrying, trying to come up with a way to let the public know he has the best tasting hamburgers of the three stands. "What can I do?" the owner asks himself. The man came up with an idea, so he put up a sign that says: **I have the best tasting hamburgers in town!**

Well, it didn't take long for the owner of the hamburger stand next door to see the first one's new sign and start worrying about the fact he would need to do something to compete with this guy. "But how can I beat this guy and let everyone know I have the best tasting hamburgers?" A week or so later, the second owner is seen out in front of his establishment erecting a new sign which says: **I have the best tasting hamburgers in the state!** That'll get their attention he thought smugly to himself as he struggled with putting the ladder back in the shed.

Now it was the third owner's turn. He needs to do something or he will be out of business soon, because ever since the owners of the two other hamburger stands put their signs up, he began losing customers. He figured he needed a new sign to compete with them, but he *wondered* what he should put on it. The first sign said he has the best tasting hamburgers in town, and the next one said he has the best tasting hamburgers in the state, what's left? A couple of days later there appeared a sign over the third hamburger stand. The sign said: **Come on in, we've got the best tasting hamburgers on this street!**

I sure like stories like this because they really get a message across. You don't have to be a brain surgeon to know how spirituality works. The biggest message I get from this story is to keep it simple! This story also proves you can accomplish things by worrying about them, but it probably won't be to your advantage in the long run. Why not? Because the first two owners are now back to worrying over their businesses again. All they accomplished was bringing on themselves more and bigger worries. That's what worrying gets you, more of the same; like begets like.

The same rule applies for wondering too. Keep miracling (or wondering) and see what you get. Simply, you'll receive more miracles (and wonder). Through miracling you gain new freedom and lose the fear of having to solve difficult situations. After practicing miracling for a while, you may wonder why you didn't try it sooner and what other problems or situations you can apply this to. You may even wonder if you've found one of the secrets of life. I'll let you in on something, and you won't have to wonder very long on this one. It *is* one of the secrets of life! I would tend to believe the third hamburger stand owner was putting some spirituality into his thought process because all he did was *wonder*, and then it came to him.

Another thing about the action of worrying is that once you're at the point of worrying over something, you've taken yourself out of the fast lane of your soul's journey. If I'm worrying about something, this immediately tells me my footwork is done, and I've gone far enough. To keep worrying over something past the finished footwork is to send a lot of mixed messages out into the universe. Worrying is a state of being and creative process, just the same as wondering is. Stay focused on the positive one (wondering) and you'll get to sit back and let life come to you, instead of the other way around.

Additionally, I've noticed when people begin worrying about something, they start making contingency plans. What are contingency plans? They're different backup plans just in case something doesn't happen the way they expect it to. When I was in deep financial difficulty and worrying about how it was all going to work out, the following happened: I sat at my desk and thought, "Let me see, I sold the hot rod and the motorcycle, so I don't have those assets to fall back on anymore. I can't cut expenses in the other areas because they're down to bare bones already, so what else can I do to get myself out of this mess I'm in?"

I gave myself a pretty good headache trying to figure a way out, yet I kept at it. I got out the credit cards and looked to see how much I could borrow off them. That wasn't feasible, so I looked at refinancing my office building again. Can you see where all these contingency plans were getting me? No where. They were just giving me a bigger headache than the one I had an hour before.

As I've discovered, when I'm in a worry mode and I'm sitting there trying to come up with contingency plans just in case I have to do some retreating, I have to ask myself one simple question: Where's my faith in God? If I truly turned this over to God in the first place, I wouldn't be putting myself through all the worry and its consequences. I use this as a yield sign when I'm coming up with contingency plans. It's at this time I need to get me out of the way. I need to quit *worrying* about how I'm going to fix it, and start *wondering* how God can.

Once you've done all you can, then it's time to leave the results in God's hands. Once you've put the creative forces of the universe into motion (your footwork), it's time to *be* patient and *be* ready for the results. Don't have expectations other than expecting that it will work out. Not having expectations as to the how of it frees you from having tunnel vision, which forces you to focus on only one way it could happen.

After questioning how strong my faith in the Higher Power is, I need to look around and make an assessment of things. If I'm experiencing apartness from God, Life, or Love, who moved? Not them that's for sure; it's me who's moved. I may not have necessarily moved away from Life, but I definitely didn't move toward it. I may have moved in a way that puts up a wall which blocks full and open communication between us. The wall I've erected is a wall of worry, which is a negative state of being. The only way to remove this blockage is to start wondering what He can do to fix the situation.

I rarely find myself worrying about things anymore. Why would I need to? It always seems to come back to these eight words: *Either God is everything or He is nothing!* Suprisingly, just today I had a situation where some worry popped into my mind. It struck me as an unusual feeling, because it's been quite a while since I've worried about anything, but then again, it's been a while since I've had to go to the dentist. Now this was one area of my life where I didn't include God. I've had some bad experiences with dentists in the past, and I've never been in much of a rush to keep in close contact with these people.

A Journey of Remembering

My teeth have never been good since I was young, so I've made many trips to the dentist to go under the whining drill. I won't lie, I usually put off going to see the dentist until I absolutely have to, which means trouble and pain for me, and lots of money and smiles for the dentist. As usual I put it off again, but thankfully it wasn't to the point of being critical, but it was close. Since my appointment was scheduled for a few weeks ahead, I was able to put it out of my mind for a while, but as D-day got closer, I found myself worrying about it. Not good.

My mind begins to take off with me when I worry about something. For instance, the needle they use for Novocain injections goes from being a couple of inches long to more than foot. And the drill bit would be the envy of Texan oil drillers going for black gold a mile down. It's not really that bad, but it sure gets close. Well, the date of my appointment arrived, and I found myself on the way to his office. As I'm tooling down the highway, wishing I were going in the opposite direction, the thought popped into my head, "Quit worrying and start wondering!" So I did. Now that's a tough one to do when you're getting your face drilled on in less than half an hour, but I managed to keep at it.

It was going a lot better for me even after I signed in and sat down in the waiting room. I grabbed a magazine to read so I could keep my mind occupied. That worked for a short time, until out of the backroom comes that dreaded high speed whining of the drill, and the dentist yelling for more suction! My prayer activity went into high gear after hearing that.

Shortly after this episode, I'm called in for my turn in the chair. I soon find myself laying flat on my back looking up at the water spots on the off-white ceiling tiles. The dentist comes in and puts a little Q-tip with some pink stuff on it against my gum. I *knew* what that was all about. That four-inch needle (I was able to get the length of the needle down a bit through prayer) was next. With the Q-tip a distant memory of only ten minutes, the dentist comes back in the room determined to get the ball rolling.

"Open wide and tilt your head this way," he prods me. I could see the needle coming my way and just before he stuck the needle in my mouth, he says, "Better say a prayer" and I respond, "I'm way ahead of ya, Doc, way ahead!" The rest of the appointment went well, and I only drooled for an hour or so afterwards. I chuckle to myself now when I remember those words just before the needle, "Better say a prayer." Do you think that was by accident? I don't think so. I took it as God saying, "Don't worry Nate, just wonder more often."

This journey of enlightenment we're all on takes persistence and patience. God didn't give us willpower for nothing. Willpower aimed in the right direction can be one of the greatest assets in your spiritual tool bag, but as with anything else, not using it properly can lead to all kinds of side-trips on your journey which will be filled with worry and doubt. Just as with my trip to the dentist, it took much less mental energy to quit worrying and start wondering than if I persisted in worrying myself sick. As with worrying, I get the full consequences of wondering too, such as the reward of wondering why I didn't apply wondering to the problem sooner. I couldn't use the excuse that I didn't know if it would work, because I've used it many other times; it just didn't dawn on me to use it in this case.

Do you see a little "coincidence" here? Just as I'm writing about worrying and wondering for this book, I get a life experience of them both. God does work in mysterious ways, His *wonders* to perform. That's what I meant about seeing, feeling, experiencing these little miracles in your daily life. They even come in a trip to the dentist. Thinking back to years ago, I would have missed these wonders completely because of my being so self-centered, which wasn't putting me on the fast track to enlightenment. I would've been in survival mode and when I get into survival mode, I ask only one thing, "How can I survive this one?" It's such a pleasure to be out of that. Thank you, God.

CHAPTER 21: GRACE IN OUR LIVES.

"Short arm needs man to reach to Heaven. So ready is Heaven to stoop to him." - Francis Thompson

Basically, what we've been discussing here in these last couple of chapters is the action of God's grace in our lives. What is the grace of God? Trying to define grace can be a very slippery thing. It's not one of those somethings a person can put a finger on and say, "Here it is, right here." In defining grace, I would have to say it's the love of God in action. Since love is the culmination of all the attributes of God, which entails compassion, trust, forgiveness, truth, humor, justice (as in fairness), joy, and all the other aspects of God, grace seems to be the force behind it all.

For me, God's grace is not necessarily defined as being in just the good things that happen in my life. The grace of God has been in those areas where it seemed He was nowhere to be found. In retrospect, I look back and see the darkest nights of my life is where His grace shined the brightest. His grace brings humbleness to me because at the very times I'm cursing Him out, He only shows His love and compassion for me. These are the times it's proven to me how He not only shows compassion and love, but also loves unconditionally no matter what fit I'm in the process of throwing.

God doesn't have to forgive any of the things we do which might be labeled slanderous toward Him, because God *is* forgiveness. We can't harm God, nor can we insult Him. He would be a very small God indeed if you believe you can offend Him.

It is we humans who have a hard time with forgiveness. When forgiveness is rarely shown to ourselves for the mistakes we've done to others, we reciprocate in kind. We won't forgive those who've harmed us, and in so doing, we've created a never-ending cycle for ourselves; a cycle consisting of resentment, fear, and distrust. We can't break this cycle on our own. It will take the grace of God to break it, simply because we're so filled with hurt and anger that we won't be the first to forgive the harm done to us. We can't forgive something that's been done to us if we can't understand the reasoning behind it. And so we begin to be like the dog chasing his tail. We just keep on going around and around.

I believe this may be the unforgivable sin that's talked about in the Bible (though I don't believe it's unforgivable by God, nor is it a sin, as has been preached over the years). Let's use a little common sense here. Do you really believe God is total unconditional love, but won't forgive certain acts? Do you think God could be so offended by us as to pitch a fit and say, "No, I'm not forgiving you for this one?" I'm sorry, but come on. God must be a very small being if He feels that way.

Because we can't, or won't forgive on our own resources, we stay in motion on a never-ending merry-go-round of hurt and pain. Until we quit the circle, God's grace can't enter; it's us who keeps Him out. It's the ultimate "Catch 22." We can't receive or experience forgiveness until *we* first express it, and because of our over-inflated egos we won't express it first, because in our minds they hurt us first. So we remain stuck: day-after-day, month-after-month, year-after-year, and lifetime-after-lifetime. As soon as the cycle is broken by an action taken on our part, then the act is forgotten. In essence, there really is no unforgivable sin. This so-called sin is just an action that results in stagnation of our enlightenment, and the only cure for this is God's grace and love.

I would like to share with you this poem I wrote almost twenty-five years ago. This was probably the darkest night of my life, my "Catch 22". I think this is a good place to share it because it was and is God's grace in my life.

A Journey of Remembering

"The Child That Cries Within"

There are no tears to feel or see; just pain and hurt.
This you can believe!
Pain and hurt breed more of the same. What is this I feel?
Is it just a game?
I don't dare tell a soul because they won't understand.
No one cares, no one to lend a helping hand.
No one knows the real me, but that's no sin.
So alone I go on living and cry within.
The pain affects every mood, every emotion,
and every decision. It's the child within crying out,
"I don't understand this confusion!"
I pray no one sees this because they'll laugh or criticize.
So I never let it escape, I bury it deep to keep it from
wondering eyes.
It never ceases, nor subsides! What do I do?
I cry within and say "Good bye."
No one hears and no one sees, because they don't care to see
the child cry within me.
Even if they try, they'll never truly know, because I'll never
let it show.

    I chose to put this poem further into the book than right at the beginning so you can better appreciate the grace of God in my life. He's brought me a long way since this dark poem was written. In many ways it was only because of God's grace that I could arrive at this point in my journey of enlightenment. His grace continues to this day in allowing me the true experience of grace by being able to express it toward you and others.
    Grace is available to all, but not all will choose it, at least at this time. They *will* find the grace though in their own time of enlightenment, whenever that may be. Grace comes in two parts. First,

A Journey of Remembering

it is available to anyone of us because God has no favorites. The second part of receiving grace in your life is you have to be receptive to it when it comes. From the outside it looks like grace only belongs to a certain privileged few, but in reality it's available to all of us because we're all one. When one of us receives God's grace, we all receive it. Do you have the eyes to see this?

Many will look but will not see, because God's grace is not something you see with your physical eyes. Grace is something that's felt and experienced within your very being, your very soul. You'll know it when you experience it, you'll experience it when you feel it, and you'll feel it when you contact God. God isn't at the end of the journey of your enlightenment; He's *in* the whole process of enlightenment itself.

God understands your journey of enlightenment. For your sake, He's the one who made all this possible. And so through that, don't you think we could learn to cut ourselves and others some slack in the forgiveness field, and show some grace ourselves? Isn't it funny so many of us believe God is all powerful and nothing can top Him, yet we put ourselves *above* (as in being more powerful) Him by not forgiving those who've harmed us, when He already has? This begs an answer to another question. How are we supposed to receive God's grace when we think we're *above* the very Being which grace comes from? Think about it; it just doesn't make any sense.

Once I was able to get my ego in check (by God's grace again) I was able to better receive grace by the spiritual parameters He's set up. To first experience or receive grace, one must first ex-press grace. The same principles apply here as when we were talking about compassion and letting go of the ball back in Chapter 18. To get, one must first let go.

This is in essence what we've been doing on this journey of enlightenment. We've been finding out what has been blocking the grace of God from entering our lives, thus making it whole again. What happens when grace enters your life? If it's already entered yours, you don't need me to tell you, because you already know. But for those of you to whom the grace of God seems to be a distant concept, I may be of some help here. Have you ever heard the saying,

"When you're living right, things go right?" This is having grace in your life. Now it may not be the right way for other people, but if you're happy and know you're on the right path (even though there may be times when you question it) and things just seem to be falling into place all on their own, then you are experiencing grace in your life.

We don't need to make it any more difficult than that. Using some more common sense here, don't you think the path of enlightenment would and should be joyful, not some rutty road you trudge down? Wouldn't you think it would be like an adventure a kid might go on when he's out in the woods playing? Isn't the child really making the adventure up as he goes along discovering new and fascinating things? Sit and watch children playing in the woods some time, because they have much that reminds us of the way it used to be, and can be again. You'll envy them for their sense of wonder, their sense of improvising as they go along, their carefree attitude, and their being able to just go with the flow.

I can remember playing outside on the warm summer evenings growing up. We'd play "Seven steps around the house" or maybe a game of flashlight tag, it didn't matter. It just seemed we were going to live forever, despite what everyone was telling us. And that's the great part of God's grace in our lives; we're still able to just have fun.

Sometimes in the spring, but always in the fall, we throw a big party at our cabin in the woods. It started out as a celebration of sorts, like when we got the land the first year. The next year we had a party to celebrate getting the cabin roughed in, and also my son Jedediah's high school graduation. The next year it was my daughter Heather's graduation party. After that we just liked having a big party in the fall. Lots of people show up for the sake of being able to be a kid again, at least for one night. We get the grills and deep fryers out and cook up lots of food. After everyone has their fill and the sun has set, we start a couple of big brush piles on fire, which I've piled up the preceding summer.

After it gets good and dark and the fireworks have been blown off, we break out the flashlights and off we go to play tag. Most everybody joins in, from five or six year olds, to people in their forties and fifties. We all have fun even after we've been running in the woods at night (and I'll tell you right now, it's not one of the smartest things to do). There may just happen to be a branch sticking out, or a tree stump found by doing a somersault over it. When we get back to the bonfire, we all laugh and talk about the great adventure we've just been on. You'd think we just took a trip to outer space the way some of the people talk. They are so filled with enthusiasm and vigor, one would think they were only ten years old again and could live forever. And guess what? They are ten years old again, and yes, you do live forever.

 As we all sit around the fire, telling new stories or reliving past ones, I get a real profound sense of grace in my life. I look into the eyes of the friends and family sitting around and I see no major cares or worries. They seem to be in a different dimension. They're all relaxed and just enjoying the moment, as I am.

 As I look around the fire I see my son Travis with his wife and their kids, actually having fun with his dad; so different from the way it used to be. I know there were times in the past when I was drinking and doing drugs that Trav wished I'd never come home again, because he wanted all the hurt and pain to go away, but today this is much different; he no longer runs and hides from me. Not only does he stop in to see me or call to see if he can help with anything, we worked together in my business for some time.

 Then there's Heather, my little "black eyed pea" (that's what I used to call her when she was real little, because she has the blackest eyes I've ever seen.) She was always the quiet one through all the misery I created. She was the last one to forgive me. She didn't need to say the words, I just knew it. After I got divorced from Wendy (their mom), Heather wouldn't even come out of her room when I'd stop over. If she did happen to come out, she wouldn't say "Hi." Sure it hurt me, but I was able to let God take care of her because I couldn't undo the damage. I'm not exaggerating when I tell you that everytime I'm with her, I get tears in my eyes for being able to be a part of her life again, this time in a positive way. Thank you again God for your grace!

 Next, I see Cassandra sitting by the fire. She's a lot like her mom, so laid back and taking it easy with life. She doesn't run from it, nor does she fight it. I was able to keep my promise to Cassandra and buy her a horse which she always wanted since she was old enough to talk. She's such a horse nut and I love it. I've always admired her openness, like the time she found my cigarettes which accidently fell out of my coat pocket (you see, I never smoked in front of my kids until after I sobered up). She came running up to me, holding them out in front of her and gave them to me. She looked up to me in a wonder of sorts and said, "Dad, I thought you quit doing drugs?"

    I was dumbfounded for two reasons. First, I was glad she felt free enough to ask me the question in the first place, and second, this was the first time any of the kids mentioned anything about my drinking and drugging. I reassured her I quit doing drugs, but I still smoked cigarettes. I would quit them too, when the time was right. It's hard to explain to a child of six or seven, that quitting drinking and doing drugs was enough to handle for the time being. Anyway, she was happy I didn't go back to drugs, and she literally went skipping away like she didn't have a care in the world; she found out everything was going to be okay.

    As we are all sitting around the fire, I pick out my former wife, Wendy (believe it or not, she's now one of my best friends). I look into her eyes and wonder how she survived the fourteen years of hell I put her through! I sit there in total disbelief that she would even want to be seen with me again, because some of the things I did to her were nothing less than pure evil. She and Vickie get along famously, which also makes me sit in disbelief and wonder. A former wife and a present wife aren't supposed to get along that well (at least that's what I've seen in other people's relationships). She's been my biggest teacher (a master) of forgiveness, and nothing less than that. She's expressed to me the true meaning of loving someone in spite of whatever harm was caused; she's a true being of forgiveness in its truest sense.

    Then there sits Jedediah, my oldest child. He's turned into a real gentleman. As I watched him in the firelight, sitting with his new wife and their daughter Grace, I can't help think back to the time when he was so sick. He was only two years old when he got deathly ill, and we took him to the hospital. This little boy was actually dying of thirst.

A Journey of Remembering

No matter how much we gave him to drink, he couldn't get enough. On top of that, he was putting out way more than he was taking in. That's when we found out he had juvenile diabetes.

What a devastating blow that was. I prayed to God to give it to me, and spare him, because I didn't want to have him start out life with such a thing hanging over his head. But he's been coping pretty well with the disease, and I leave him in God's hands as there's nothing I can do about it. I joke with him about how he has to take shots to live (his insulin), and I had to quit taking shots (as in whiskey) in order to do the same.

Then lastly, I find Larinda, or Rindy. This is Vickie's daughter from a previous relationship of hers. Rindy was about two-years-old when she and her mom came into my life. Rindy's father and Vickie broke up when she was still a baby. She never got to know her biological father, even though he lived close by. Apparently he wasn't into being a dad, so he just wrote Rindy off. He never even bothered to call or write to her. She came into my life about the same time I sobered up. She never saw the drunken me, which is a blessing in itself.

After Vickie and I were together for some time, she asked her mom one day if she could call me Dad, because she always called me Nate before this. Vickie was sure I wouldn't mind and told her to go for it. It wasn't too long afterward that she just started calling me Dad. It was about this same time I was in the process of letting Autumn and Benny go. God, I was mixed up inside. Here I was, a father who was letting go two of his children, yet at the same time taking on a new one. It was such a confusing time for me, but it felt so right. She has blessed my life in more ways than she'll ever know; thank you God, for sending her my way.

I thank God all the time that all these people are in my life, and have forgiven me for the harms I've caused them. Remember when I said a little while back you don't see grace with your eyes, you feel it inside? That's what I feel when I am with these very special people. It's simply the action of the outpouring of grace in all our lives and that brings you a lot of gratitude for His love and compassion.

Grace is elusive until you quit trying to catch it. You have to be open to it, if you are to receive it. Like the other states of beingness we've previously discussed, you also have to possess it in order to give it away. I want to leave this chapter now with one last thought. Whenever I see someone going through hell with something in their lives, I say to myself, "But for the grace of God, there go I. I've been to hell. I bought the T-shirt, the hat, and the coffee cup! Thank God I made it through in one piece."

A Journey of Remembering

CHAPTER 22: AN ATTITUDE OF GRATITUDE.

*Gratitude is not expressed with words,
gratitude is expressed with actions.*

For me, gratitude is an expression of thankfulness. It's a thankfulness that comes from deep within and is expressed outward toward God and my fellow human beings who've joined me in this journey of remembering. Not only have they remembered my soul, but they've remembered their own as well. The reason I say gratitude is not expressed with words but with actions is because when one is truly grateful for something, there are no words to be found which can truly express what one feels inside. How does one put into words the appreciation he or she feels when someone or something has acted in part to save your life, and helped to make it a joy at last?

How many times have you seen on television or read in the newspaper about someone saving the life of another person, and the person who's been saved from death is trying to express their gratitude? I've seen it many, many times, and it's been said by the person who's saved that saying "Thank you" just isn't enough. It doesn't even come close to being able to express the appreciation they feel inside. That's the same way I feel when I experience God's grace in my life. Saying thank you is nice, but it just isn't enough for me. I'm writing this book out of a sense of gratitude for the Higher Power having been there *all* the time, and also in the hope that these written words will help and be a guide to others struggling to find their way on their own journey.

A Journey of Remembering

    This journey I'm on is *not* the only way to finding a state of serenity, joyfulness, and peace. There are many, many ways, but I do believe there are commonalities we share on all these journeys. We only need to be open to the many possible ways God's grace can enter and act as a beacon in guiding us home.

    Have you ever noticed when a person is feeling lost, whether physically or spiritually, they become so absorbed in finding out where they're at and how to get unlost, that they miss out on all the great things going on around them? Once you're able to get your bearings, you then experience a sense of peace that allows you to not struggle anymore. You gain a sense of knowing the search is over, and you can now enjoy the many things you've been passing by.

    I spend a lot of time in the woods, and I'd be a liar if I were to say I didn't get lost a time or two. Honestly, it's been more than a couple of times. Upon realizing I'm lost, the first thing that sets in is panic. My mind starts screaming, "Where in the hell am I and how do I get out of here?" After being able to work through that (with a little prayer or two), I try to determine how I got turned around, and what I'm going to have to do to find my way back. It's been my experience that going back the way I came is not the best course of action, because that way got me lost in the first place. What I need to do when I'm lost is to find a way *forward* which leads to safety. Since going backwards has been ruled out as an option, there's only one option left.

    When I find myself lost in the woods and I'm plotting a course forward, I find something to focus on up ahead to help me get out. I suppose about this time you're wondering why I don't use a compass to find my way out of the woods. That is a valid wondering. My answer to that would be I never planned on getting lost, so why take a compass? That very reasoning is what gets me, and a whole lot of other people into trouble while taking a walk in the woods or on the spiritual path. We think we don't need guides or aids since we don't plan on getting lost on the journey.

    A word of advice here: Just because you've been hunting in the same woods for ten or fifteen years (and think you know it like the back of your hand) doesn't mean you shouldn't bring along a compass. This goes for spiritual matters as well. It's very easy to get lost or turned around when not using a guide of some sort. God didn't give us the ability to make and use compasses and other aides for no reason.

I can remember a time when I went bow hunting for deer with my nephew Timmy. I told him I was going to take a walk around this beaver pond about half a mile back in the woods which I had hunted around many times before. I told him it should take me about an hour or so to make it around the pond, and I would see him back at the truck at dark. Telling Timmy where I was going was the only smart thing I did. I took off on my merry way just enjoying the beautiful surroundings. I got to the beaver pond and proceeded to go around it, but yet it seemed that I was continually going around it. The more I tried to go around it, the worse it got. I soon found myself smack-dab in the middle of a huge watery marsh.

I was wading through water up to my arm pits at times. This is not a good thing to do when one is wearing chest waders, because once the water gets in and fills them up, you sink like a rock and there's no escape if you can't reach a branch or something to pull yourself out. As my waders started to fill up with water, the saying came to mind: "Bubble, bubble, bubble, no more trouble!" It's funny how one has a sense of humor when facing death. Knowing I was in serious trouble now, I needed a plan of action to get myself out of there. I didn't care at the moment that I was lost; I was focusing on saving my life. After assessing the situation, I figured I could kind of hop on the soft, murky bottom as I reached for a bog that was floating nearby. I then used that one to hop to the next, and then onto the next, until I was able to reach firm ground.

It was nearly dark when I finally reached solid ground. I had to concede to myself that I was hopelessly lost. Looking back at the way I came, I knew there was no way I'd be able to get through that alive again. I'd damn near bought it a couple of times back there, and I wasn't going to make that mistake again. As I sat down on a log to rest and have a smoke, I put my head in my hands, closed my eyes, and said a little prayer. Way, way far off in the distance I could hear a cow mooing, and then a dog barking. My ears stood at attention then because I didn't know there were any farms in the area. This gave me hope, and something to go on.

A Journey of Remembering

After about another hour of wading through more swamps and beaver ponds, I was able to make out the silhouette of a barn in the moonlit blackness. I figured I was still lost, but at least I wasn't *that* lost anymore. Before reaching the farm, I found a dirt road that didn't look familiar at all, but I took off walking down it anyway. After another half hour of walking, I finally came to another road, and this one I knew. Man, oh man, I really went out of the way. From where I entered the woods to getting back to the truck was probably a good six mile trek.

Resigning myself to a long arduous walk, I set out on the journey back to the safety and comfort of my truck. It was going to be a tiring walk, but at least I wasn't lost anymore. I experienced the feeling of being found, and that's when I began to enjoy the scenery around me, which wasn't much because it was now totally dark. I did notice though the countless bright stars on that cool, crisp fall night, and I could hear the hoots of an owl in a far off tree. My expression of gratitude to God for helping me get through this one was to go out the next day and buy a nice compass and pin it to my hunting suit!

So it is with being spiritually lost; once the sense of being found sets in, one doesn't say to himself, "I think I'll be grateful now." You're just grateful, and when you are that full of gratitude, you'll find a way to express it somehow. You won't be able to stop yourself, because you'll just start doing grateful things, and in the end, you will have discovered the beingness of gratitude.

I'm going to share with you a story that describes this better than I can. It's about a man who was walking along the beach the morning after a terrible storm had rolled in off the ocean. As he was walking along the beach, noticing all the debris which washed up on the shore the night before, he spied someone up ahead of him. He could see someone walking up to the water's edge and then back to the sand dunes; they kept doing this repeatedly. The man hurried his gait so he could further investigate what was going on. As he got closer he could see it was a little girl and she would pick up something off the sand dune and proceed to take it to the shallow edge of the ocean. Once in the water, she would gently set it down in the frothing surf. "Very intriguing," the man thought to himself.

A Journey of Remembering

The man just had to find out what was going on, so he approached the little girl to ask her what she was doing. As he walked up to the little girl, he noticed hundreds of thousands of starfish lying all over the beach. He asked the little girl what she was doing. She replied, "All these star fish were washed up on the beach during the storm last night, and I'm putting them back into the ocean so they can live." Methodically she turned around to get another one and said, "They'll surely die here on the beach." The man thought this was a nice thing to do, but what would it matter? So he asked her, "That's all good and well, but there are hundreds of thousands of star fish lying here, and you won't be able to put them *all* back in the water to live, so what does it matter?"

The little girl bent over and lovingly picked up another starfish, walked out into the salty surf and gently returned the starfish back to its home. As she was standing in the water watching the starfish swim away, she turned to the man and said, "What does it matter? It matters to that one!"

This is perhaps my favorite story of all time. This story is not about words of gratitude, it is about actions of gratitude. I tend to believe this little girl was grateful for having survived the storm herself, and in a child's way found an expression of that gratitude by helping others who couldn't help themselves. She was able to express gratitude in a way that was special only to her. When she was expressing her gratitude, she didn't care what others might say or think about her actions; it only mattered that she was able to do it. Did you notice she wasn't focused at all on the ones she couldn't help? She kept her focus on the ones she could save, because it *did* matter to each and everyone of those she was able to put back in the ocean.

Mother Theresa put it all into perspective when she was asked by a reporter why she devoted her whole life to feeding the starving masses of India. The reporter remarked she would never be successful in feeding them *all*. Her reply was simple, "I wasn't sent here to be successful; I'm here to be faithful." For whatever reason, she was a true being of gratitude and compassion. She shied away from publicity for herself due to the fact that she wasn't doing it simply for the honors she could reap. She was doing it because of the simple fact that it did

A Journey of Remembering

matter to each and every individual she was able to help. That's what gratitude does. It's not for self-glorification; it's for the returning of something that has been received in the past.

This is why I feel so blessed. I am able to share with you my life's journey of enlightenment and remembering so far, because it *does* matter to some, and that's enough for me. Even if it only matters to one other soul, is that not grand? It boggles my mind to think of how far advanced we'd be as a civilization if even one half of us were living a life of gratitude and compassion! There would be no more wars, there would be no more ultra rich and destitute poor, and there would be no more crimes against humanity such as we've experienced in the last fifty years!

How many "little girls on the beach" or "Mother Theresas" do we have to experience before we wake up and realize we as a human race are lost? We've had, and continue to have, shining examples of love and compassion in human form as beacons to show us the way. Yet we choose to go the other way and lay waste to our environment and all living things which inhabit this earthly home. We've been sent wake up calls for thousands of years now starting way before Jesus, and yet we still don't get it!

The human race as a whole is pretty much ignorant of the situation we've put ourselves into, but there is change in the air! Can you feel it? It's so thick you could cut it with a knife. Many people today are waking up to the fact *we're* the ones who've done this to *ourselves* and God's not the one to blame. We're the ones who've fouled our air and water, not God. We're the ones who think the almighty dollar is what's going to fix us, not God. We're the ones who say you have to believe in God in such and such a way and if you don't, we'll kill you! God didn't make us do this to ourselves; we did it all with our own free will.

We don't learn from our past mistakes, but yet we beg God to solve all the world's problems when He didn't make them in the first place. Who do we humans think we are? Why do we keep shitting in our own bed and yet expect God to clean it up? He's provided all the things we need to live comfortably, all of us (man, woman, and child included from every corner of the planet). Why, we have enough wealth in this country alone to share with the world and still have some left over. There's enough food throughout the world to feed everyone a couple of times over, yet we sit on our asses and watch them starve to death! Where's our humanity? Where's our gratitude?

I've come to believe that if people don't appreciate what they've been given, and in turn show an appreciation of it by sharing it with those less fortunate, they'll no longer have it. That applies to countries, too. It's that simple. According to the spiritual parameters I've set out previously, to try and hoard something is the fastest way to make it disappear. By the same token, the more we're able to give away (or express our gratitude), the more we'll be supplied with the very thing we're giving away. How do you get more gratitude in order to express it more? By simply *being*; by being more of the same which initially gave you the gratitude in the first place. If you find something that works, keep doing it.

My best days of spirituality are the days I've been able to share it with someone else. Soon after the sharing or expressing of gratitude, comes more gratitude and more feelings of having to share what I've come to experience, which in turn brings more opportunities to share, which in turn brings more gratitude. See how it all comes together? Then you throw in a prayer or two of gratitude to God for having the opportunity to play a part in the Great Plan, and it makes the gratitude come even more. It just keeps snowballing. The more grateful you are, the more opportunities you get to show it, which makes you even more grateful, and on and on.

Earlier in this book, I mentioned that one of the greatest prayers ever prayed, is a prayer of gratitude, I would like to get into this further now. What is a prayer of gratitude? Simply, it's a prayer of thankfulness for His being here and helping us get along on this journey of enlightenment. It's a prayer of thanks for the love and compassion He shows us at the times we need it most. It's a prayer of thanks for putting just the right people and circumstances together to aid us on our journey to get to know Him while forming a loving relationship with Him. And lastly, it's a prayer of knowing, experiencing, and remembering. Once you've thanked God for doing what you couldn't do for yourself, you've removed all doubt in your mind as to why a certain thing happened in a certain way. In short, you've experienced a part of God.

Let me explain this a little more. Let's assume you said a prayer of thanks to God for accepting you for just who you are at this very minute. This is a prayer that is full of certainty; it's a statement of the fact you've received His acceptance. Now, how could you pray in thankfulness if you haven't already experienced gratitude? You can't. So a prayer of gratitude is not a prayer in which you are *wishing* God would accept you. A grateful prayer is not something in which you're expressing a *want* or a *desire*; it's a statement of how you're being. When you're in a state of *being* grateful, it eliminates the needs, wants, desires, hopes, longings, or other similar condition.

Being in a state of gratitude *proves* you have no wants, needs, or desires as it applies to the very thing you're grateful for, or else you wouldn't be there. You can't be grateful for something, and still want it at the same time. You can't be in two opposing states of being at the same time. You'll either have a feeling of gratefulness or you'll have a feeling of want or need. Gratitude is a feeling of completeness while a feeling of want or desire is a feeling of emptiness. How can you have both as it applies to the same thing? You can't, it's impossible. So it is with all states of beingness; either you're in one or the other, there's no in between.

Remember, you have great powers of creation at your disposal. The very thoughts, words, and deeds *ex-pressed* by you are created in your reality. This is not a game of switching words around. Those words expressed and acted upon bring about exactly what they are. You can take the long route of creation by going through something, seeing it wasn't exactly what you hoped it would be, and then decide to do something different which will get you back to the desired results in the first place. We do have a shortcut in creation by eliminating all this groundwork that went beforehand and just go to a state of beingness; in short, just be there.

So it is with a prayer of thankfulness or gratitude; we've eliminated the state of wanting and gone right to an expression of a feeling of already having. I know this sounds a little too simple, and a little confusing at times, but we humans need to learn to do things differently, because the way we've been doing things is not ending in concert with our good intentions.

Our societies of the world will advance light years when or if we can go from the state of wanting all the time, to a state of being. Wanting something has proved it will get you nothing, except more wanting. We've got to get to the state of being where there's no want, and the only way to get there is with God's help. This United States of America didn't come about by some people over in England *wanting* something different. They got off their asses, picked up their guns, and told England to go to hell. Now, that's a state of being!

Slavery didn't end in this country by people *wanting* it to end. Most people were sick and tired of the state of being that made it okay to own and abuse other people. They made a statement of how they didn't want to be anymore and then took the steps to make it right. They made great sacrifices and were willing to die for their beliefs, thus changing the world's consciousness. This is what it's going to take to physically change the things in this world that aren't working for the advancement of the human soul. This world needs an attitude of gratitude, because anything short of this will not do.

CHAPTER 23: A JOURNEY WELL TRAVERSED

"A man with God is always in the majority."
- John Knox

Once a person has obtained and is living a level of enlightenment, one will be living quite differently. It will appear to the enlightened one as though this was not a conscious choice (at least in the sense where a person just decides one day to live differently all of a sudden), because this form of living will be something that has happened seemingly out of nowhere. Yet if one were to examine it closely, this different way of living will have been based on countless different choices one has made along this journey of remembering.

One day, this person notices that he's arrived at the destination of his soul's enlightenment. One doesn't arrive at this point and say, "I *think* I've arrived." When one has reached this destination, a person of enlightenment will *know* it, because they will be experiencing and expressing it. An enlightened soul will never believe upon reaching this destination that it's the end of the journey. The enlightened knows it's just the beginning.

The only thing that has ended is the pursuit of external things with which to fix him self. Enlightenment is seeing and experiencing that there's no pursuit, and there never was. The enlightened one knows there was nothing to pursue from the start because he's had everything all along. All the material objects are put into their proper perspective, and in that way they were and are all just means to an end. They are to be used as guiding instruments taken from the spiritual kit

A Journey of Remembering

we were provided with at the beginning of the journey. Since the enlightened soul will have quit the pursuit (it was just an illusion anyway), he experiences there was really nothing to pursue in the first place, because the whole journey was about remembering; the remembering of the soul's quest from the beginning.

This journey we're all on is an individual quest for meaning and purpose. Have you ever sat and pondered the meaning of the word individual? I looked up the definition in the dictionary and it says this: *that it is not divisionable without loss of identity.* In other words, if we're *not* an individual, then we've lost our sense of identity or soul's purpose. Yet, this is exactly what the religions of our day profess to do; to give people a sense of identity in respect to God. But how can they give a sense of identity when they've taken away the individuality of the people by impressing on them their own attitudes, beliefs, and fears? They can't; this is counter-productive. In actuality, this is leading them *away* from God instead of *to* God.

There's another interesting thing about the word individual. If you break the word down, what do you have? You get in-dividual. Remember me saying all answers come from within? With*in* is where you find enlightenment, because that's where you find God. I hate to burst a lot of people's bubbles, but God is not hanging on some cross, or in some ornately adorned building which has set up all kinds of rules and regulations governed by fear as to how one should think, believe, and act. An enlightened soul doesn't need all this external pomp and circumstance. It's in being an *in*-dividual and going inside oneself, where one experiences God.

One would think that by shunning the external and becoming an individual, one would lose all sense of identity in respect to the other souls around them. This is not true. In reality, going within is where one finds union *with* other souls and finds they're not separated from others, but joined *with* them. An enlightened one not only knows, but also experiences the fact of the oneness of all things, which includes all other souls.

We're all individually here as vital parts of the Whole. We're all part of the Great Individual. God could no sooner deny a soul that came from Him, and is a part of Him, as we could deny one of the ten

A Journey of Remembering

fingers on our hands. It just can't be, and an enlightened one knows this. They've come to the realization that what they do to another, they do to themselves; we're *all* a part of the Greater Whole.

An enlightened one also knows that the circumstances and events of his life happen due to the total union of all souls, not because of the singleness of one soul within itself. Singleness of the soul proves a separation of one thing from another, and that can't be. We're all so interconnected it would blow your minds to know the true reality of it all. Singleness of the soul provides for another separation too; the separation from God.

We cannot ever be separated from God, for in the instant of this happening, the soul would cease to exist. Our souls would cease to exist because all sustenance comes from within, not from without. Taking this a little further, if our souls would cease to exist, what do you think would happen to God? Common sense says He would cease to exist, which we know is not possible, because He told us He always was, and always will be! In reality, the journey of the soul is re-union, reunion with other souls and in the end, reunion with God. How do you fix a separation of two things? Be re-membering them back together. *So in order for us to have that long sought after reunion with God, we must remember.*

Once one has reached enlightenment, the battle is over even though there didn't have to be a battle in the first place. One finds a true place of contentment and serenity, with love being the energy that drives it all. What more is there to do, but experience more of the same? An enlightened one neither runs, hides, nor fights for anything, because they're now experiencing a state of pure "being." Therefore the words, "I AM THAT I AM." While in this state of beingness, everything will come to you; all you have to do is just be something and it's so. It's in this way we find true communion with God; we've remembered. We're partners in this creation. Did Jesus not say: "Ye also are Gods" (John 10:34).

Did God not also say in an opening verse of the Bible, "Let us create man in our image, in our likeness?" (Genesis 1:26) Can you discern the full impact of this, my friends? These may be the most powerful ten words ever written down on paper. Have you ever *really*

A Journey of Remembering

looked at those words, studied those words, questioned those words, or applied those words? Here are a few things to wonder about. Who's the "us" He's talking about? What does it mean to create? Whose image are we created in anyway? What is the likeness He talks about? Now there's something I'll leave to you to wonder about.

Now we're coming full circle in this enlightenment journey. By being true to thineself, we not only experience ourselves in this journey of enlightenment, we experience all others in the process. Do you think the other people we've met and had interactions with on the journey through this lifetime were all by accident? No, you've brought them to yourself in order to experience some facet of your soul's enlightenment and theirs too, all to facilitate a remembering.

Now maybe you'll be better able to understand what Jesus meant when he said "love your enemies, bless them that curse you" (Matthew 5:44). It's mainly through our enemies (whether that means other people, or that shadow side of our own personality) we find enlightenment. God bless them for being there, and doing for us what we couldn't do for ourselves. How could we have experienced our own wholeness if we didn't have anything to reference it to? We couldn't.

With God's help, we've created this whole lifetime of drama (cast, characters, and sets) with the sole (or soul) intention of not only knowing who and what we are, but also experiencing it in its totality. When I reflect back on those relationships of the past that seemed so bitter and hurtful at the time, they were there for the single purpose of finding the true me, to help me remember.

Likewise, those we have interactions or relationships with, have attracted you in the same way and for the very same purpose. We're actually like magnets drawing each other together for a common purpose. What power would act as a magnet to draw something together like this? Love! Love is the magnet of the soul, and fear is the repellant. Do you think people were drawn to Jesus because of His good looks? Apparently not because there's nothing mentioned on this subject. If He had Robert Redford's dashing good looks, we would've all heard about it and he'd probably be all over T.V. commercials and plastered on billboards trying to sell us something.

What Jesus stood for can't be bought in any store, but it can be purchased for a price. That price includes courage, faith, belief, trust, and open-mindedness. A being of love knows nothing of inconvenience, dishonesty, doubt, or fear. A being of love expresses nothing but compassion and kindness. They have no bias, prejudice, or agenda. In simple terms, their love is unconditional; it has no conditions, it just is what it is.

To sum things up, I would like to share with you this last story. It's about a stonecutter and a mountain. The story goes like this: One day a stonecutter is toiling away at the base of a mountain. While taking a much-deserved break, he ponders his lot in life. "I would like to be so much more than what I am," he says to himself. He figures his lot in life doesn't seem to matter to a whole lot of other people. Being a spiritual person he turns to God and asks Him to turn him into the mountain, as he figures the mountain is so much more powerful than he is. He's worked his whole life removing stones from this huge mountain, yet standing at a distance, one can't even see what he's accomplished. Now, if he was the mountain, people would surely notice him.

And so it came to be; God turned him into the mountain. "Now I'm something people will have to notice!" he pridefully said to himself. But as he sat there doing nothing, because that's what mountains do, it became apparent to him that people still didn't really care about him. They figured he was just a big pile of rocks standing in the way of progress. He sat there and pondered some more as to how to turn this around. He needed to be something people would notice, something that wouldn't be taken for granted. So he prayed to God once again. As he was talking with God about what a mistake he'd made, he noticed the sun up above shining in all its brilliance.

"Ah," he thought, "now that's what I need to be, I need to be the sun. None of these people will be able to ignore me if I were the sun!" So he asked God to turn him into the sun, to which God gladly obliged. He liked his new role in life. Everyone could admire his great brilliance now, until the clouds started coming by. "What's this?" he questioned himself. "I'm brilliant and powerful and yet these clouds

A Journey of Remembering

block me out!" Realizing he'd made another mistake, he entreated God to turn him into the clouds he felt were more powerful than the sun. And so it came to be.

As he was floating above the earth, enjoying his new status being the clouds, something was brewing up ahead. As he floated along, guess what happened next? He floated smack dab into the same mountain he'd been a stonecutter on before. Now, he was enlightened! He then knew and experienced all that there was for him to feel. Being the stonecutter was what he was supposed to be. It was not about power and glory, it was all about the process of the journey he was on, and he thanked God for indulging him.

This story sums up the whole journey of enlightenment. Journeying around is part of the process, but in the end, it all comes down to just accepting who you really are, and then journeying forth from there. We don't need to be all these other things, because in being them, it brings us right back around to where we started.

My friends, you have now traveled with me on my journey. In my expressing of this journey, it's become a part of yours in the same way yours has become a part of mine. We've not only become more whole, we've become part of the Whole (which is life, love, or God). He's been with us the whole time, and will continue to be. I do know we'll be together throughout all time.

I'm going to take this opportunity to express my gratitude to my fellow travelers who've joined me in my soul's journey of remembering and enlightenment, because without you I couldn't be. Thank you also to the Great Spirit for this chance to be with you and share the most wonderful adventure of this lifetime. Even though there were many moments where You and I didn't see eye to eye on things, I am humbly grateful for the understanding, compassion, and unconditional love you've shown me in spite of my many actions of defiance. I should have expected no less, because that is what you are, perfect love. *Now I remember! I do love and thank you all!*

I would like to finish this writing with a poem I've written for the Spirit as I understand Him/Her today:

A Journey of Remembering

My Gift to Thee

What shall my gift to thee be?
My gift shall be wrapped with honor and reverence,
to be bound by my love of thee.
The bow will be made of appreciation and love,
tied with the patience that was shown me.
This gift is made of joy because that has replaced the
sadness of the past.
My gift that is bound with love will forever last.
This gift is made of gratitude, gratitude for the love and
kindness that you've always shown me.
This gift is bursting with joy; I don't know if the binding of
love can contain thee!
Forever I have waited for this moment to come.
Forever I will take pride in a gift well done.
What shall my gift to thee then be?
My gift to thee then, is me.

A Journey of Remembering

ABOUT THE AUTHOR

Nathan Whiting has called central and northern Wisconsin home his whole life, but that doesn't mean he hasn't ventured forth to some of the spiritual centers of the world. Nathan has just returned from a spiritual sojourn to Machu Picchu, located in Peru. Adding to his list of spiritual adventures are two visits to the Mayan Chichen Itza pyramids in the Yucatan region of Mexico, and multiple visits to the natural spiritual centers of the western United States, including Yosemite, Bear Tooth Pass, and Glacier National Park, along with various adventurous side trips to western ghost town haunts.

Nathan is one of eight children and has seven children of his own. He is the very proud grandparent of 12 grandchildren and counting. They keep him laughing and enjoying the small, simple things in life, like sitting on the couch reading a picture book, or sojourning forth into the woods on a discovery mission of what may lie just over the next ridge.

After cleaning up from drugs and alcohol in May of 1981, he struck out on a spiritual quest to find meaning and purpose to his life. Just being sober and straight was not enough for him; he wanted to keep drinking (spiritually speaking) from the top shelf, just as when he would find himself sitting long-faced in a bar and requesting the best the house had to offer.

Early on in recovery he was posed with this very question: "If you only drank top-shelf in your drinking days, why would you take less than top-shelf in sobriety and

A Journey of Remembering

recovery?" Those simple words set him on a quest for an answer to the ultimate question every soul on this planet yearns to know: *What am I here for?*

Nathan is currently enrolled in college and is on the home stretch of receiving his BA in Psychology from a midwestern university. Approximately four years ago he received a Certificate of Ordination as a Nondenominational Spiritual Minister, and has had the honor of officiating at various weddings, funerals, and "whoopee parties."

For further information and correspondence, visit Nate at: www.ajourneyofremembering.com.

A Journey of Remembering

Also Available from Summerland Publishing

Angel on my Handlebars is the true story of the 50 days it took Patricia Starr to pedal 3,622 miles across America. Patricia was a 67-year-old woman in short shorts and Hanes Pantyhose riding a $600 bicycle with a kickstand and a fuzzy seat cover. Many of the days during the ride stretched between 100-120 miles.

Patricia Starr is a concert pianist, and was crowned Ms. Senior California at age 69 in 2006, and Ms. Senior Nebraska in 2008.

Price: $19.95   ISBN: 978-0-9795444-8-4

"Lucky Me", narrated by a rescued dog named Rocky, provides a guide to children and parents looking to add an animal companion to their family. Illustrated with full color photographs by the author, Rocky and his friends walk us through what a humane society can offer to animals, and what every animal guardian should know about caring for and keeping their new family member safe.

Price: $14.95   ISBN: 978-0-9795444-9-1

That religions profoundly affect our lives in innumerable ways, no one is likely to dispute. Disagreements emerge, however, when we attempt to evaluate those effects, and when we attempt to determine religion's proper place in our lives, in our society, and in our troubled world. Wouldn't it be worthwhile for everyone to think through our religious traditions one more time, from the beginning? Isn't it possible to resolve some of the issues involved in a manner that is less militant and more intelligent? **"Comparing and Evaluating the Scriptures"** by Paul Fink will give readers the opportunities they seek to develop clear answers to these questions and more.

Price: $16.95   ISBN: 978-0-9795444-3-9

Order from:
www.summerlandpublishing.com, www.barnesandnoble.com,
www.amazon.com or find them in your favorite bookstore!
Email Info@SummerlandPublishing.com
Summerland Publishing, 21 Oxford Drive, Lompoc, CA 93436